CLASS AND SKILL

Other titles in the Cassell Education series:

P. Ainley: *Young People Leaving Home*
P. Ainley and M. Corney: *Training for the Future: The Rise and Fall of the Manpower Services Commission*
G. Antonouris and J. Wilson: *Equal Opportunities in Schools: New Dimensions in Topic Work*
M. Barber: *Education in the Capital*
L. Bash and D. Coulby: *The Education Reform Act: Competition and Control*
D. E. Bland: *Managing Higher Education*
M. Booth, J. Furlong and M. Wilkin: *Partnership in Initial Teacher Training*
M. Bottery: *The Morality of the School*
G. Claxton: *Being a Teacher: A Positive Approach to Change and Stress*
G. Claxton: *Teaching to Learn: A Direction for Education*
D. Coffey: *Schools and Work: Developments in Vocational Education*
D. Coulby and L. Bash: *Contradiction and Conflict: The 1988 Education Act in Action*
D. Coulby and S. Ward (eds): *The Primary Core National Curriculum*
L. B. Curzon: *Teaching in Further Education (4th edition)*
P. Daunt: *Meeting Disability: A European Response*
J. Freeman: *Gifted Children Growing Up*
J. Lynch: *Education for Citizenship in a Multicultural Society*
J. Nias, G. Southworth and R. Yeomans: *Staff Relationships in the Primary School*
R. Ritchie (ed.): *Profiling in Primary Schools: A Handbook for Teachers*
A. Rogers: *Adults Learning for Development*
B. Spiecker and R. Straughan (eds): *Freedom and Indoctrination in Education: International Perspectives*
R. Straughan: *Beliefs, Behaviour and Education*
M. Styles, E. Bearne and V. Watson (eds): *After Alice: Exploring Children's Literature*
S. Tann: *Developing Language in the Primary Classroom*
H. Thomas: *Education Costs and Performance*
H. Thomas with G. Kirkpatrick and E. Nicholson: *Financial Delegation and the Local Management of Schools*
D. Thyer and J. Maggs: *Teaching Mathematics to Young Children (3rd edition)*
M. Watts: *The Science of Problem-Solving*
M. Watts (ed.): *Science in the National Curriculum*
J. Wilson: *A New Introduction to Moral Education*
S. Wolfendale *et al.* (eds): *The Profession and Practice of Educational Psychology: Future Directions*

Class and Skill

Changing Divisions of Knowledge and Labour

Pat Ainley

CASSELL

Cassell Educational Limited
Villiers House
41/47 Strand
London WC2N 5JE
England

387 Park Avenue South
New York
NY 10016-8810
USA

© Pat Ainley 1993

All rights reserved. No part of this publication may be reproduced or transmitted in any form or by any means, electronic or mechanical, including photocopying, recording or any information storage or retrieval system, without prior permission in writing from the publishers.

First published 1993

British Library Cataloguing-in-Publication Data
A catalogue record for this book is available from the British Library.

Library of Congress Cataloging-in-Publication Data
Applied for.

ISBN 0-304-32681-X (hardback)
     0-304-32679-8 (paperback)

Typeset by Colset Private Limited, Singapore
Printed and bound in Great Britain by
Dotesios Ltd, Trowbridge, Wilts.

Contents

Outline	vi
Acknowledgements	vii
1 Introduction – Understanding Rapid Social Change	1
2 Two Approaches to the Question of 'Skill'	5
Quality	5
And Quantity	10
The Emergence of Skill	14
New Technologies, New Skills	19
3 What Has Happened to Social Class?	25
Marx on the Middle Class	25
The Way We Were	29
Beyond the Great Divide	33
Towards Mass Multiskilling?	37
4 'Skill Shortages' and Class Cultures	44
Whose 'Skill Shortage'?	44
Information Society	50
Cultural Differences, Economic Similarity	56
The Resurrection of the Rough	62
5 Popular Perceptions of Social Class	67
In the Middle – Between the Snobs and the Yobs	67
Working for Yourself in the Enterprise State	72
Education and the Middle Class	77
Class Consciousness in a New World Order	81
6 Conclusion – Skills for Survival	86
Bibliography	94
Name Index	100
Subject Index	103

Outline

This is a short book that aims to deal with a lot. The argument in places is therefore fairly dense. It is hoped that this will not put off the general reader for whom the book is intended. This outline indicates its scope and order.

The perennial English obsession with social class is approached from the tangent of a new and more specialized preoccupation with defining the notion of skill. Both words are changing their meanings under the impact of accelerating social change and the latest applications of a new information technology. Computer screens render explicit meanings that were previously taken for granted, at the same time reinforcing the illusion that all definition can be reduced to mathematical formulation.

Current debates in the social sciences have been profoundly affected by the apparent collapse of the Marxist paradigm for understanding society in terms of social class, against which even other, opposing versions of events tended to be constructed in the past. The 'post-modern' acceptance of the relativism of competing explanations of reality places a question mark over whether any one explanation is possible any more (if it ever was), as well as over previously accepted notions of history and progress.

The introductory chapter having indicated this context of debate, Chapter 2 takes two perspectives, from gestalt and behavioural psychology respectively, to look at opposed definitions of skill before casting back into history to indicate the skills of the past and then looking forward to the skills that may be required in the future. Asking 'What has happened to social class?', the third chapter also looks back to the origins of the class concept in the modern form of society created by the industrial revolution, especially as it was applied to the middle class in Victorian society and then to what happened to the classes so defined from the Second World War to the present.

The notions of skill and class are then combined in Chapter 4 to examine the 'skill shortages' held by many to be responsible for the failure of Britain's repeated attempts at modernization. It asks to what extent this failure is attributable to cultural factors and how these are changing. Popular perceptions of what is happening are then drawn from a range of sources in Chapter 5 to bring to the fore recent social changes, especially as reflected in the provision of education. Margaret Thatcher's period in office is seen here as a watershed marking the transition from one type of society, characterized by traditional divisions of knowledge and labour, to an 'enterprise state' with a new mixed economy of privatized state and subsidized private industry. In this new situation divisions of skill and class no longer map out divisions in society in the way they once did. The state, with its new, franchised form of administration and contract culture, therefore steps to shore up the old divisions, especially through the education system. At the same time far greater changes in the rest of the world also affect people's perceptions of their own situation.

The prospects that continuing economic crisis will accelerate historical and even climatic change pose the problem of creating skills for the future – a problem that is addressed practically in conclusion.

Acknowledgements

To Sheena Ashford for giving so much time to a detailed reading of the text and for her suggestions and criticisms, not all of which were taken but all of which were well meant. Also to Professor Ken Roberts for his encouragement to 'give it a whirl' and likewise to Naomi Roth at Cassell.

Most of all, to Beulah and Adam for their patience.

Trade winds are blowing,
Blowing around me,
While all around me,
What do I see?

Hatred and jealousy,
Brotherhood's dying.
Love is the answer
But nobody's buying.

Good people turning bad,
Exceptions are so few.
The winds are blowing,
The choice is up to you.

We're caught in the trade winds,
The trade winds of our time.

Ralph McDonald and William Salter, 'Trade Winds', as recorded by Maggie Bell on *Queen of the Night*, Polydor Records, 1974. © Cyril Shane, Artesia Music. Reproduced with the permission of BMG Music Publishing.

Chapter 1

Introduction – Understanding Rapid Social Change

Conceptual models, even when incorrect, are useful to the extent that criticism of the model may point to new theoretical developments.

(Bateson, 1978)

Is it possible any longer to understand the rapidity of social change and to present it in the comprehensible form of a theory of society and a history of its relations to the natural world? Most social science no longer attempts such a task, nor is it nowadays written within the traditions of such an approach. Generally sociology is intimately concerned with undertaking more or less applied research at the behest of policy-makers and is written for the benefit of other social scientists. Within social scientists' community there is no longer much agreement on the meaning of the social classifications that used to be the key terms of their craft. In particular, analysis of society in terms of social class has been largely abandoned in favour of description by measures of social status. There is no longer any attempt to discover the forces that move societies along the path of history. Indeed, most such efforts are regarded as discredited. In part this change of approach and of sociological method is due to the belief that in recent years society has changed in some fundamental and irreversible ways.

Certainly at the beginning of the last decade of the twentieth century there were changes enough abroad, with the ending of the Cold War following the collapse of the state capitalist form that communism took in Eastern Europe, to raise hopes that the terrible history of wars and revolutions initiated in 1914 might at last be buried. Above all, the possibility of catastrophic nuclear war has been lifted, if only temporarily, for the first time for more than forty years. Might not the science and technology upon which the West had relied to create the affluence envied by the rest of the world now be used to confront the real problems facing humanity? For, instead of instant destruction, longer-term but more insidious threats loom on all sides, from the damage being done to the environment all around to new and so far incurable diseases working within. Both have been stirred up and unloosed by the rapidity of social change. Yet the science looked to for a solution to these threats to further human progress merely seems to exacerbate many of them – from the conquest of disease permitting exponential population growth among the impoverished majority of the world, to the technology that spreads cancerous contamination from its chemical and nuclear plants. Just as humanity's mastery over nature has been revealed as illusory by the uncertainties of the climatic change human activities have triggered off, so science's claims to produce technological solutions to human problems no longer seem credible.

Or is it the casting aside of old beliefs in a future state of human perfectibility that makes for the present predominant mood of unease? For this is the essence of the real change that seems to have occurred: it is the acceptance that, despite society having reached a new stage of its development, this achievement is the outcome of previous tendencies that have continued unchanged. Moreover, it is also widely accepted that no further change is possible, or at least that future changes will only be incremental additions to the present state of affairs. The convergence of political belief in the mainstream British political parties as well as in formerly antagonistic international ideologies sustains this notion. This reduces government of society and management of the economy to accommodation with the inevitable trade cycles upon which the system of international competition that generates national wealth depends. The autonomous market mechanism is accepted – at least in theory – on all sides as essential and there is disagreement only upon how far it should be modified and its effects mitigated. Meanwhile, the repeated cycle of booms and slumps to which the market is prone is seen to be unavoidable and as natural as the seasons. This fatalism contrasts with demand management of the economy after the Second World War, when the relentless switchback was at least temporarily overcome. Even before then most people had been employed during the upturns. Now the whole security of permanent employment is being lost, as even many employed people are part-timers on temporary contracts. Today the permanent unemployment of millions is tolerated as a structural necessity and governments have dropped their previous shared commitment to full employment as a goal of economic policy. Thus the hopes held since the Enlightenment, that progress and increasing rational control over society and the economy were possible, if not eventually inevitable, have been abandoned.

It is this context that makes the claim that there has been a fundamental transformation in society and the world different from similar assertions that have been heard so many times before. For there is always a tendency for any social formation to regard itself as the final product of its history, if only because its rulers, having put themselves into power, seek to keep themselves there by declaring that everything will remain the same from now on. This is the case even for such paradoxical societies as our own modern ones, which have committed themselves to constant advance but only on condition that what are widely regarded as their essential values of freedom and democracy (however loosely defined) remain unaltered. The universal extension of formal freedoms and representative democracy, together with rising standards of living for all members of society, was previously held to account for the transition to what was popularly presented as a meritocratic society. This was supposedly ruled by technocrats recruited on the basis of their expertise, not by virtue of their privileged birth. It promised an end to poverty as an affluent and apolitical working class was incorporated into a plural society of individuals. Unlike totalitarian dictatorships, which imposed a unifying ideology to justify their rule, this was an open society in which individuals could make up their own minds pragmatically between competing versions of the truth. The model was a universal one, so that even the communist countries, which came to be ruled by a new bureaucratic class, were seen to be converging with the capitalist and technocratic West as mass-produced goods rendered everything everywhere increasingly homogeneous and indistinguishable. Similarly, this model of development promised the former colonies modernization via industrialization, to achieve the shared goal of catching up with the most advanced economies.

All these ideas were common currency by the late 1950s, when the American sociologist Daniel Bell first announced 'the coming of post-industrial society', but the ideas have gathered new force with the decline of factory production in the West and the predominance there of service industries. New technology now appears to offer the prospect of a second industrial revolution, with computers substituting for brain in the way that steam had previously replaced muscle. Information thus supposedly succeeds capital as the source of wealth and power. This post-industrial 'information society' has been welcomed by those who celebrate individuality set free from the constraints of the past. The supersession of old styles in art and architecture is associated by them with the ubiquity of advertising, which ransacks the costume cupboards of history to present a collage of styles designed to sell the latest information compressed into instant images. According to this 'new times' version of recent history, such 'post-modern' culture is created and patronized by an elite core of administrators and technicians who control access to vital information.

To its critics, this plural society of specialized markets presents itself as an apartheid world in which everyone talks but no one communicates because the basis for any shared community has been lost. Indeed, the critics allege that the impossibility of even conceiving, let alone communicating, any notion of reality that is not partial and fragmentary is denied by those for whom history has become mythology, science has become magic and morality has become purely contingent self-calculation.

Other commentators deny that any fundamental change has occurred at all. They suggest that capitalism has merely undergone another of its successive transformations from the unbridled free-market competition with which it began, through the agglomeration of cartels and monopolies concentrating plant, machinery and raw materials into fewer and fewer hands and bringing together more and more workers in factories organized around the relentless rhythms of the assembly line, to a new phase of 'post-Fordist', 'flexible', 'disorganized' or even 'moribund' capitalism. In this latest phase, financial speculation and trading in 'futures' that may never be realized take precedence over the actual production of commodities. This notion of a quantitative shift in economic organization shares certain features in common with the proponents of qualitative change to a new and different type of society. Whether they are labelled 'post-capitalist', 'post-industrial' or just 'a new regime of flexible accumulation', both conceptions imply a major change in the class structure of developed societies. For without factory production concentrating masses of workers together, the classical proletariat has dissolved into a competing crowd of individuals. Optimists see here an opportunity for reskilling the entire workforce with the new conceptual skills required for efficient use of computer-controlled technology. A new system of mass higher education and training is thus called for, raising the expectations and performance of the entire working population. Pessimists detect, contrariwise, a new division between a securely employed, multiskilled core and a much larger periphery of insecure, semi-skilled, part-time labour to be used and discarded into habitual unemployment as required by the latest demands of production.

At a popular level discussion about the nature of the changes that have or have not occurred in modern society is posed in terms of skill and class. These two terms are related not only by the divisions of knowledge and labour from which they both derive.

New skills are held to be necessary for the transition to a modernized economy making the fullest use of new technology, while 'classlessness' is the social prescription promoted by government to achieve this economic goal. The meaning of the term 'skill', which was perhaps always essentially indefinable but which was widely used as if it was fully understood, has thus changed from its origins in manual craft. Similarly class, which was once a word that had a very precise meaning that everyone understood but no one talked about, has now also come into common parlance, but no one knows what it means any more.

In England the changes in society that brought about this new use of old words are associated with the Thatcher governments that seemed, to both their supporters and their opponents, to mark a watershed between the old society and the new. Since 1979 both statistical evidence and everyday experience of life, particularly in Britain's cities, attest that extremes of wealth and poverty have increased. This reversed the previous slight narrowing that it was accepted had occurred since 1945. It thus seems ridiculous to assert, as Mrs Thatcher repeatedly did towards the end of her reign, that a transformation in society had been achieved that had done away with the traditional and notoriously ingrained distinctions between the social classes. However, this was the theme taken up by her chosen successor in his proclamation of the goal of a classless society of equal citizens that, remarkably, found some popular reverberation at the time. The same goal has long been held by the opposition parties, though they do not see that it has already been completely achieved but are committed to reaching it themselves by slightly different means. The idea that such a transformation has already occurred coincides with the claim that there has been a transition to a new type of post-modern society. Like the French theorists of post-modernism who deny there can be shared objective knowledge about anything and especially about society as a whole, Mrs Thatcher more straightforwardly asserted, 'There is no such thing as society.' If this really were the case, it would be impossible to establish whether any change had occurred, let alone the nature of that change. And because of the new uncertainty about the old idea of progress, it seems problematic whether such knowledge would be of any use. For despite the emphasis upon individual opportunity, events seem so far beyond individual control and comprehension that all such discussion is rendered futile.

Contrary to this prevailing mood, this book argues that there are things that individuals can do to change the situation and that they begin with an objective understanding of society and its development from our subjective position in it. Such an overall comprehension is possible, though it is not easy. As a contribution to the necessary understanding of rapid social change an explanation is proposed through an examination of what has occurred in recent years to two key factors in the sociological debate – class and skill.

Chapter 2

Two Approaches to the Question of 'Skill'

Of what cannot be said thereof one must remain silent.
(Wittgenstein, *Tractatus*)

QUALITY

Attempts to define skill originated in psychology and there are two approaches to the question in the psychological literature. These perhaps reflect two different but simultaneous ways in which the brain deals with reality, but they are also influenced by the cultural biases and scientific commitments to different 'schools' of their advocates. The difference between what Rosenbrock called the causal and purposive myths of scientific explanation 'stems ultimately from the fact that the former builds up the world from simple, self-sufficient entities, while the second begins from the opposite extreme, from ultimate purpose' (Rosenbrock, 1990, p. 114). Their combination has been called 'intuition' (Cohen, 1981). Which approach is adopted in order to define skill might seem a purely technical decision but it soon becomes apparent that it is one upon which rests deep philosophical divergence. Above all, it is a question of where skills – and ideas – come from: are they innate in the individual mind so that they can be measured in performance along the lines of an intelligence quotient, or is their source outside any one individual, however accomplished or however blessed with inherited talents? If the latter is the case, then skills are not measurable in the same way in their individual performance but are recognized and developed as part of the culture shared by skilful individuals. They are acquired by apprenticeship and through tradition and are not then the property of individuals but belong to the practical knowledge developed in society through its division of knowledge and labour. In this case, the itemized competencies demonstrated in the performance of a skill become dissolved into the larger whole of which they are but a part.

David Pye, who was professor of furniture design at the Royal College of Art, illustrated this last approach to the question of skill. Writing in 1968 on the nature and art of workmanship, he noted the rising interest there then was in design, but the neglect of any corresponding interest in work. Yet what he called workmanship – or craft, in the case of 'workmanship of the better sort' – was necessary not only to realize any design but also so that the design could exist in the first place, for designers can only specify techniques and uses of materials that workers have already invented. 'Design', he wrote, 'is what, for practical purposes, can be conveyed in words, numbers and drawing; workmanship is what, for practical purposes, cannot' (Pye, 1968, p. 2). Pye refused to use the word 'skill' because he saw it as 'a thought preventer' (p. 24). 'It does not assist useful thought because it means something different in each different kind of work' (p. 23) and 'Workmanship in different trades differs so widely in its basis as well as its practice, that the only common factor and the only common means of generalization in all the different branches of craftsmanship is the element of risk' (p. 12). Whether a task is undertaken by hand or using a machine, for instance, is irrelevant to assessing this element of risk. Pye gave the examples of a dentist drilling a tooth with an electric drill, a pretty risky operation, and someone drilling a piece of wood with a hand drill. In the latter case, unless you are fool enough to break the drill, you only have to keep on turning the handle to complete the job. The source of power is therefore also irrelevant to the risk involved. By contrast, in the case of the dentist, 'The essential idea is that the quality of the result is continually at risk during the process of making' (Pye, 1968, p. 4).

In what Pye called 'the workmanship of certainty' the end-result is exactly specified beforehand and then the work is carried out so that there is no possibility of the worker spoiling the job, or of improving upon it, even accidentally, except perhaps by deliberately 'throwing a clog in the works', or sabotage as it used to be called. In the contrasted 'workmanship of risk' the result is not predetermined but depends on the judgement, dexterity and care of the worker, so that the job can be spoiled at any moment. However, Pye indicated two ways in which workers constantly tend to reduce the risk and increase the certainty involved in any task, so that 'the workmanship of risk in most trades is hardly ever seen and has hardly ever been known, considering the ancient use of templates, jigs, machines and other shape-determining systems' (Pye, 1968, p. 5). Tools and machinery thus tend to develop so as to take over from their fallible human operators, especially as they become more complex and sophisticated than the simpler tools they replace. Pye's example here was printing compared with using a pen:

> The first thing to be observed about printing, or any other representative example of the workmanship of certainty, is that it originally involves more of judgement, dexterity and care than writing does . . . but all this judgement, dexterity and care has been concentrated and stored up before the actual printing starts. Once it does start, the stored-up capital is drawn on and the newspapers come pouring out in an absolutely predetermined form with no possibility of variation between them.
>
> (Pye, 1968, p. 5)

The other way in which workers or artists – makers in both cases, and the words originally had the same meaning, as for example in artisan – can ensure that the result of their work corresponds as closely as possible to their preconceived idea of what they want to achieve is through developing habits of work. This is also a major economy of effort, so that the result is attained with the least possible physical exertion and so that conscious attention can be directed to what is essential and away from repetitive and routine operations that can be completed unconsciously.

Pye's 'uncertainty principle', as it can be called, has been explained at length because it offers a guiding thread through the complicated discussion of 'skill' as variously defined in the modern training debate. It offers a criterion, though by no means a quantifiable or exact one, for distinguishing between 'bad' and 'good' work – the degree to which the work corresponds to the original and ideal conception of it. This is a mark against which any human creation must always fall short, for, as Pye explained, 'All workmanship is approximation to a greater or lesser degree' (p. 13). Pye's principle also affords a similar qualitative indication of skill levels in the contemporary arguments surrounding skill acquisition and loss, with regard to the effects upon the workforce of new technology. To reiterate: 'In the workmanship of certainty there is no rough work. The perfect result is achieved directly without preliminary approximation' (p. 16). Thus, 'The workmanship of certainty is, simply of its nature, incapable of freedom' (p. 19). For 'Free workmanship is essentially of the nature of a sketch' (note to Plate 4).

David Pye is not widely known now, except perhaps among furniture designers, but his views agree with those of the more august, although more obscure, philosopher of science, Michael Polanyi. Even though one suspects that he is not read so much as he is referred to, Polanyi's is a name to conjure with in the debate about skills. This is partly because his approach emphasizes the importance of unarticulable and pre-rational tradition in the transmission of skills down the generations. It therefore appeals to those for whom education and training are limited to learning by example, which meant, Polanyi explained, 'to submit to authority' (Polanyi, 1969, p. 53). Such educational traditionalists and authoritarians never tire of repeating, almost as a mantra, Polanyi's dictum that 'There are things that we know but cannot tell.' Yet the idea that more can be thought than can be expressed is not unusual; it is described, for instance, by Blumenberg in his monumental *Legitimacy of the Modern Age* as 'the basic principle of all hermeneutics', especially as, he adds, we think of more than we can say 'still more in after-reflection than in forethought' (Blumenberg, 1983, p. 86).

Polanyi, like many of the intellectual émigrés to the West in the years after 1945, wrote from an explicitly anti-Marxist position. In his major work, *Personal Knowledge: Towards a Post-critical Philosophy*, first published in 1958, he sought to put the defence of 'the open society and its enemies' on a more secure footing than Popper (1966) was to leave it with his fallibilist conception of knowledge, in which theories are understood as hypotheses subject to revision. Polanyi shared with the present-day philosophers of post-modernism an objection to the attempt made by Marxism and other 'closed' ideologies to contain all knowledge in one overarching theory that explained everything. Like them, he saw totality in systems of thought as leading to totalitarianism in politics. Unlike them, he did not use Popper's principle of the relativity of all knowledge, subject as it was to falsifiability by scientific experiment, to escape into a world where all grand theories or 'meta-narratives', including all scientific explanations, are equally invalid and reality is thus essentially unknowable. Rather, Polanyi grounded scientific knowledge in 'a more primitive level of articulation, relying only on rudimentary or at any rate quite informal logical operations' (1969, p. 84). This 'informal intelligence' or 'understanding which we cannot put into words . . . is continuous with the inarticulate faculties of animals' (p. 90). Even though, unlike animals, human beings have speech in which to communicate at least something of what they understand, 'owing to the ultimately tacit character of all our knowledge, we remain ever unable to say all we know . . . [and] we can never quite know all that is implied in what we say' (p. 95). Thus, 'the inarticulate always has the last word' (p. 71).

Polanyi's justification of scientific knowledge borrowed from gestalt psychology and in particular the work of Kohler with apes (see Kohler, 1968). The use of tools, which Kohler saw in his celebrated monkey reaching for a banana with a stick, is therefore also important to Polanyi. 'An object is transformed into a tool by a purposive effort envisaging an operational field in respect of which the object guided by our efforts shall function as an extension of our body. My reliance on it for some end makes an object into a tool, even though it may not achieve that end' (Polanyi, 1969, p. 60). The subject/ape is bound into an active and intentional whole/gestalt by the connection between tool/stick and object/banana. 'The act of personal knowing can sustain these relations only because the acting person believes that they are apposite; that he has not made them but discovered them. The effort of knowing is thus guided by a sense of obligation towards truth by an effort to submit to reality . . . like love' (pp. 63–4). Rather than advocating a philosophy of authority to justify unthinking tradition, Polanyi might better be described as advocating the method of discovery learning so disliked by educational authoritarians. Similarly, his effort to discredit a Marxism that had become rigidified into a dogmatic and closed ideology points towards a way of opening materialist systems of thought to the reality they seek to describe adequately if never completely to contain.

These ideas were more succinctly expressed in Polanyi's better-known article on tacit knowing in the *Review of Modern Physics* in 1962. Here Polanyi picked up on Wittgenstein's questions about the meaning of knowledge: 'When do you know how to play chess? All the time? Or just while you are making a move? And the whole of chess during each move?' (Wittgenstein, 1968, p. 59). Characteristically Polanyi took as his examples the more physical and less cerebral activities of swimming and riding a bicycle. In these cases, 'I can say that I know how to ride a bicycle or how to swim but this does not mean that I can tell how I manage to keep my balance or stay afloat.' Indeed, if it were possible to become aware of 'the coordination of elementary muscular acts' that make up the skill, 'its performance would be paralysed', for 'when we focus our attention wholly on a particular, we destroy its meaning' as part of the whole. There are therefore two kinds of knowing that together contribute to knowledge of anything: 'knowing by attending to' and 'knowing by relying on'. The former may be articulable and conscious but it relies on the latter, tacit knowledge, inarticulate and unconscious though it is. It is Polanyi's argument that all knowledge, including the discoveries of science expressed in the most abstract formulas, 'ultimately . . . has the structure of tacit knowledge'.

The implication of Polanyi's argument is that there is no basis for any distinction between 'higher' and 'lower' order, intellectual and mechanical skills or faculties, and that the elevation of mental over manual labour is merely a social preference for the skilful manipulation of symbols as a more respectable activity than the skilful manipulation of objects. Moreover, it can be seen that the most skills are required by those who combine what is conventionally known as mental and manual labour in their work. The most skilled are those having complete knowledge of an entire process and the ability to use understanding of working in one area to comprehend what is happening in another. Apart from very specific skills involving delicate operations in which the most complete knowledge possible of tools and materials is required, for example in traditional handicrafts, the skills most highly valued in society are diagnostic ones. Mechanics who can test and analyse engines to find and repair their faults are deemed more skilled than fitters who have passed only those tests accrediting them with the competence to fit exhausts in a drive-in centre. Similarly, the more complex the machinery or system with which a person is able to deal, the more uncertainty there is built into it and the more skill is required to set it up, if not to operate it. Thus, in computing, systems analysts who devise and test new programs use more skills than the operators who merely follow the system once it has been installed. This also applies to scientific discovery and artistic creation, work that may at the same time use extremely sophisticated equipment and involve a high degree of theoretical abstraction, often combined with creative intuition. In medical science, which deals with the diagnosis and repair of the most complex organic malfunctions, surgery is recognized as especially skilful. This is because the surgeon uses manual skills with delicate tools on sensitive material, combined with general diagnostic ability. The manual tools of the surgeon are no longer derided as they once were ('old sawbones', etc.). The proverbial brain surgeon, like the skilled mechanic, computer systems analyst, scientist or artist, combines mental ability acquired through theoretical study with manual dexterity developed by long practice. Neither purely bookish knowledge (things that can be said or read but cannot be done), nor the unformulated but tacit knowledge of the practice of a craft ('things we know but cannot tell') is alone sufficient to manage the considerable uncertainties involved in any of these occupations. The highest-order skills therefore combine mental and manual abilities, 'the marriage of intellectual inquiry and practical skill' that Rosenbrock (1977) considered made the first industrial revolution possible in Britain.

Although managers may no longer be able, as the old iron masters of the industrial revolution were, to perform all the operations of any of their operatives, they are responsible for handling the combined uncertainties of all the various activities undertaken by the organization of which they are in charge. Thus skill is generally equated with management, in so far as management is not, as Cooley (1980, p. 80) quotes a Lucas Aerospace worker as saying it so often is, merely 'a command relationship, a sort of bad habit inherited from the army and the church'. At this level skill is widely recognized as the ability to deal with uncertainty or, as it is more usually put, to take risks. In this sense information is power, as long as managers are in a position to act on the information, which gives them a comprehensive understanding of the organization they control and the parameters within which they can act. They lack the skills commensurate with their responsibilities to the extent that they lack an adequate conception of the overall functioning and direction of their enterprise within its existing constraints. Their responsibility is more than a legal or contractual obligation if what they do – or whether they are present at all – makes any difference to the conduct of the enterprise.

The belief that management or control problems can be expressed in closed forms following a series of logical steps to be solved by algorithmic procedures is often regarded as more 'scientific' than allowing room for the exercise of human judgement and skill. Yet the predominant ideal of Western science since Newton – of containing all possible information in numerical form and reducing all possible interactions to mathematical formulas – is ridiculed by Polanyi as a logical absurdity:

> We can use our formulas only after we have made sense of the world to the point of asking questions about it and have established the bearing of the formulas on the experience that they are to explain. Mathematical reasoning about experience must include, beside the antecedent non-mathematical finding and shaping of experience, the equally non-mathematical relating of mathematics to such experience and the eventual, also non-mathematical, understanding of experience elucidated by mathematical theory. It must also include ourselves, carrying out and committing ourselves to these non-mathematical acts of knowing. Hence a mathematical theory of the universe claiming to include its own bearing

on experience would be self-contradictory in the same sense as the conception of a tool would be if the tool were described as including its own user and the things to which it was to be applied.

Such comprehensive refutation has of course had little effect upon the constant effort to turn things into numbers and to elevate exactly specified quantities over indefinite qualities. This is reinforced by a dominant and long-term historical tendency within Western culture, which cannot accept differences without assigning arbitrary comparative values of more or less, better or worse, dearer or cheaper. This habit of mind has been given greater force recently by the computational powers of new technology. Computers have reinforced the widespread illusion that marshalling and reordering vast amounts of quantifiable data necessarily produces a superior picture of reality to any other that may not be so exactly expressed in numerical terms.

AND QUANTITY

Blumenberg, whose study of the origins of modern, secular society in the pre-modern, religious past has been briefly referred to, noted the vital contribution of approximation to this historical process of giving everything a numerical and thus comparative value extrinsic to its inherent worth or place in a previous magical or religious order. Objects and their qualities (size, heat, weight, etc.) could be measured and so compared in a new ranking to the nearest quantity, with 'the renunciation of the phantom of the requirement of absolute accuracy' (Blumenberg, 1983, p. 500). Similarly, abandoning the medieval ideal of knowing everything in a beatific vision of all knowledge was essential to the progress of particular sciences. Thus, 'The knowledge of the modern age was decisively rendered possible by a knowledge of what we cannot know and by the resolute concentration that made possible upon a realm that had become accessible to judgement' (lumenberg, 1983, p. 500). There is nevertheless a persistent tendency to make some particular knowledge the basis of all possible knowledge and for approximate and arbitrary measures to substitute themselves for the realities that they represent. This tendency is demonstrated very clearly in the case of an alternative specification of skill that derives not from gestalt but from behaviourist psychology. In this approach the unit of study is not the wider society or social group of which the individual forms a part, but the individual subject who 'owns' the skills in question.

Since skill cannot be demonstrated except in individual performance, this definition describes skills in terms of tasks or operations. An operation is specified by its goals, the achievement of which in a practical test indicates possession of the corresponding skill or competence. At a general level, therefore, skill is equated with the competency to complete a given task with absolute certainty of result. Conversely, inability to perform the operation indicates incompetence. At the particular level this definition reduces skill to the description of tasks or operations. To facilitate comparison between what may be dissimilar tasks, work study using hierarchical task analysis describes skills as operations that are envisaged as a nested hierarchy. Any one operation is analysable in two or more sub-operations, with nothing added or left over. The simplest possible operation thus tends towards an either/or, on/off action. Such analysis reduces complex tasks to the sum of their binary parts, and jobs are evaluated in terms of the range and scope of their component tasks.

An example of such an approach to the definition of skill was the attempt by the Manpower Services Commission in 1977 to develop an 'occupational skills inventory' or 'matrix'. The MSC's approach derived from the application of behavioural psychology to work processes and followed visits to Canada and the United States by Department of Employment officials to review the latest applications there of behavioural industrial psychology. The matrix was subsequently developed in collaboration with the Institute of Manpower Studies at the University of Sussex, the Social and Applied Psychology Unit at Sheffield University and the Tavistock Institute in London. As summarized by Moore (1985, p. 5),

> The skills inventory purports to represent skills actually required in industry and necessary to the performance of specific jobs. These skills are represented in the form of atomised 'items' of behaviour which can be referred back to the underlying 'generic skills' and grouped together into Occupational Training Families of associated skills and job clusters. Possession of these skills (referred to as 'skill ownership') is seen as facilitating labour mobility by virtue of their 'transferability' and so overcome 'labour market rigidity' (ie: trade union 'restrictive practices'). A crucial aspect of the skills inventory is that it is immediately translatable into a curriculum because it specifies in a very precise way what people are meant to be able to do (not know) in order to perform particular jobs. Also, because these skills are supposedly drawn directly from industry itself they are taken as representing what employers actually require, hence promoting employability.

There was at the time considerable doubt as to whether all possible tasks in every occupation in the economy could be accommodated within eleven training families, and whether within them the particular skills required to perform those tasks could be subdivided into their component parts. In a study of the basic issues involved by the Psychology Department of Warwick University, which the MSC financed but delayed before publishing, Annett and Sparrow (1983) questioned the grouping of itemized competences into 'occupational training families'. These were, they considered, merely 'a device for planning training programmes. They derive more from conventional wisdom than either psychological theory or from statistical analysis of actual job components.' Moreover,

> We find no basis in the psychological literature for expecting greater transfer of training between jobs within the same occupational training family than between those which have been classified as belonging to different families beyond what could be expected from an empirical determination of common elements. OTFs might even have an undesirable blinkering effect if people who had received training within one OTF were to regard themselves as unsuited to work in another.
>
> (Annett and Sparrow, 1983, p. 15)

Whether or not as a result of this report, the grand design of redesignating and reclassifying all tasks in all occupations with a view to designing a 'modernized apprenticeship for all' was abandoned by the MSC in favour of a system of modular training. This was later adopted as the ordering principle of its activities by the National Council for Vocational Qualifications.

Modular training has long been employed in adult training programmes, where retraining may only be required for one particular task from a range of occupational competences. For example, in the Road Transport Industry Training Board's modularized scheme the competence to fit exhausts in a drive-in centre is attested by the requisite module rather than by apprenticeship in all the skills of a qualified garage mechanic. Of course the route to further training is not closed thereby; further NVQ modules may be taken to build up to the level attested by the old apprenticeship qualification. The addition of new modules to old, previously accredited competences is also supposedly uniquely responsive to new developments in industry that is being transformed by the applications of new technology. Modules are normally accredited by the completion of trainee profiles. Profiles list the tasks required for completion in the test situation, whether this be at a school, college, test centre or on the job. Skills testing for guaranteed competence arguably gives credit for practical abilities untested by traditional written examinations. All trainees 'can do' at least some of the items profiled on the menu of practical tasks. Their sense of worth is thus supposedly enhanced by their achievements in a benchmark test; this contrasts with their being failed in comparison with the minority who pass traditional examinations. However, even in a list of practical tasks that are presented as equivalent to one another, certain items are recognized by both trainees and their testers alike as higher-order abilities than others. For example, in a Royal Society of Arts profile for a diploma in communications, the ability to 'read simple printed texts' is subsumed in the item 'read complex written texts'.

The same problem of lack of equivalence between tasks afflicted the effort to extend testing for certain competences to the social and life skills that formed part of the core of youth training. Here there is an additional difficulty of discriminating, recording and accrediting isolable competences in this much more diffuse area. 'Life skills' on the Youth Training Scheme (as it then was) related particularly to such work-relevant matters as 'time-keeping, discipline and the maintenance of relations with others'. However they also included 'all those abilities, bits of information, know-how and decision making which we need to get by in life'. 'Most of us', the MSC's 1984 *Instructional Guide to Social and Life Skills* continued, 'take these basic day-to-day skills for granted . . . [But] many people' lack them. Aside from the fact that it was to this deficiency in individuals that their unemployment was attributed, habits and attitudes were here dignified as skills to be tested or, rather, as competences to be registered on the profiles that were then ubiquitous in training organizations, schools and colleges. In the process they were subjected to the same routinization and particularization that characterized the same approach to technical skills. The same method of instructing and testing trainees on their social interactions by following the subroutines involved was applied to the other core area in the YTS, of 'broad based practical skills'. These were the practical tasks that were held to be common to all eleven occupational training families. They included such nebulous items as the 'ability to learn to learn'. There was an elusive search within this core for the 'general transferable skills' that trainees could carry over from one OTF to another but they could not be found because it is not that ability is transferred to different tasks but that some tasks within different occupations are similar to one another. Real transferable skills in fact represent a different order of general-level ability from the certain completion of specific tasks. The ability to learn to learn, for instance, can be acquired even by laboratory animals that get used to looking for patterns and regularities in test situations, where they perceive that their different efforts will be met with the same reward of food when they are successful.

As Polanyi had pointed out, people do not acquire a skill just by learning to perform its fragments; they must also discover the knack of coordinating them effectively. This can be demonstrated and imitated but it cannot be taught or written down. It must be discovered by an intelligent effort of the learner to integrate the parts into a whole that is greater than the sum of its parts. There is an element of this kind of knack in even the most formal and theoretical instruction, as exemplified by Wittgenstein's exclamation, 'Now I can go on!' By contrast, for a robot to carry out a task successfully, it must be programmed to perform each (binary) element of the series in the correct sequence. This is why the performance of robots, even 'creative', connectivist robots, is so limited, useful though they may be within those limitations. Competence, defined as the certain ability to complete a given task, is different from skill. Eliminating uncertainty from a particular operation reduces it towards its simplest, binary terms. Either the operating light shows, in which case press the proceed key, or it does not, in which case do not proceed – replace the whole unit or call the supervisor. The disasters to which this rigid compartmentalization are prone become plainly apparent in the case of what computer scientists call a systems breakdown. As each operation is simplified to the point of either/or, on/off certainty, coordination of the operations has to be highly synchronized. Breakdown of the system as a whole can then be caused by the failure of any one particular to operate at its appointed time and order. Once this has occurred there are very few people who still have the overall command of the process to discover and right the fault. Furthermore, the rigidities of such a system make it unable to deal with any change beyond the parameters it has been set. Since technical and social change happens constantly, and in today's society with exponential rapidity, such a modular approach to training for the future needs of industry is potentially disastrous. The piece-by-piece addition of new modules, certifying the ability to perform new operations, to old and previously systematized and accredited competences cannot lead to the control and understanding of new processes. It devalues the uniquely human skills of intuition and creativity that are irreplaceable by machinery and so often necessary to cope with the uncertainties of unprecedented change. They are lost in favour of purely mechanical, repetitive and quantifiable certainty.

The place of skills in human culture is also misconceived by this approach. Skills as a part of culture are a social question, so that the problem of so-called 'skill shortages', for instance, cannot find a purely technical solution. For skills, as Polanyi suggested, are a part of culture. 'Knowledge and organisation are properties of groups and transmitted from generation to generation by learning, not genes' (Washburn, 1978). In this respect the practical culture of an art or craft resembles the discipline of a science or other academic subject. Compared with animal behaviour, where 'social learning is important but . . . tends to be non-cumulative, modification of learned behaviour and its transmission to subsequent generations is relatively infrequent. In general the existing stock of learned behaviour is simply perpetuated' (Woolfson, 1982, note 53 to p. 95). Unlike the acquired or inherited behaviour of animals or the programmed instructions of robots, cultural information is often profoundly modified in its transmission to subsequent generations. This is why education is fundamentally unpredictable: you do not know to what use your students will put the skills and information they learn; you do not even know how the symbols (not signals, unlike in animals) that you use to communicate will be interpreted by anyone else. Like a language, human skills are modified in use; they can be extended and developed or become ossified and die. Roger Coleman saw the contemporary loss of so many practical technologies, arts and skills to automated mass production as a disaster comparable with the destruction of the tropical rain forests (Coleman, 1988, p. 4).

At an individual level, skills and the culture of which they form a part are acquired through socialization as what the French educational sociologist Pierre Bourdieu calls *'habitus'* – 'the durably installed generative principle of regulated improvisations' (quoted in Robbins, 1991, p. 83). This 'practical senses' – described by Bourdieu in the Kabyle term for 'nose', or as the English would say, 'nous' – enables individuals to respond to their situations with strategies 'embedded in the agents' very bodies in the form of mental dispositions' (Robbins, 1991, p. 109). The importance of such individual 'habits' and of the collective cultures from which they derive, both ignored by the quantitative, behavioural approach to skills and their acquisition, will be returned to in a consideration of social class. Meanwhile the two approaches to skill that have been outlined can now be applied to a consideration of the quite recent emergence of the skill question in contemporary society.

THE EMERGENCE OF SKILL

'The problem of skill', wrote Collins, 'comes partly from treating expertise as a property of the individual, rather than interaction of the social collectivity. It is in the collectivity that novel responses become legitimate displays of expertise' (Collins, 1989, p. 82). In the collectivity known as 'primitive' society, where before the neolithic revolution mature individuals were probably familiar with all the technology of their time, the division of labour was based upon age and gender. In so far as there was any division between manual and mental labour under general conditions of scarcity and with a limited development of technology, which meant that every member of society had to do some physical work at least some of the time, mental work in handing down the traditions of the tribe and the technical expertise acquired during a lifetime was the specialized function of the old, whose wisdom was universally revered. Through age-grading an individual acquired in turn and by initiation all the skills shared by the collectivity as a whole. It was only with the development of technology allowing for the production of a surplus sufficient to feed some members of society who did not have to work to produce it that the mental work of organizing the efforts of others emerged as a distinctive division of labour in its own right. The chiefs who directed the efforts of societies to greater effect at first usually took over command from a council of elders only in emergency situations, as in the Native American institution of warchiefs, but eventually came to safeguard their privileged position with an armed bodyguard of their relatives. For someone not to have to spend his life on hard labour was regarded as such a remarkable phenomenon by the working majority that the first rulers were everywhere accorded the status of god-kings who were literally not of this earth.

Previously it can be supposed – since few god-queens seem to have emerged – that the evolution of the division of labour between the sexes, which at first favoured women, had been reversed. As explained by Mary Douglas (1986, p. 76), 'Most hunters and gatherers combine a steady subsistence based on vegetable resources with unpredictable, irregular sources of wild game. Their nomadic pattern first assures the basic supplies, moving to pick up the various wild harvests as they ripen here and there. The steady tasks are allocated to women. At the same time, young men are trained to go off after the hazardous game on long treks, entailing hardship and danger.' Young men, it should be noted, were regarded as more expendable than reproductive females, whose survival was essential to the biological future of the group – only one male being necessary to fertilize several females in social conditions of group marriage or polygyny and the ignorance that must once have existed of paternity. Here the skills of the hunt were socially undervalued in relation to the essential female role of gathering basic food supplies to ensure daily survival, while the risks involved in child-bearing became the basis for a seemingly pan-Neolithic cult of mother worship. Several feminist studies (for example, Elaine Morgan's *Descent of Woman*, 1973) have also asserted the social importance of what were in all likelihood the originally exclusively female crafts of midwifery, pottery, basket-weaving, embroidery, etc. This was 'a valid division of those skills between the sexes', which, as Coleman (1988, p. 38) pointed out, 'bears the traces of a cooperative life that ensured survival in a harsh world'. Today this division is sustained in the metropolitan countries only in the remoter pockets of rural life and is not to be confused with contemporary gender stereotypes, which, Coleman added, are 'essentially urban, as are the reactions against them'.

In advanced agrarian societies the division of labour became fixed into castes. While the division of labour was simple, in terms of the numbers of different occupations, compared with today, it was complicated by these few roles being mutually exclusive and at the same time interdependent. By lifetimes of concentration upon one particular trade, handicrafts were developed to levels that modern society can still not surpass, even with all the technical aids at its disposal. Although the peasant majority in medieval society were virtually interchangeable one with another as regards the all-round skills of self-sufficient agricultural labour in which they were constantly engaged, the minority of specialists were mutually dependent upon them and upon each other for their means of life, which they could obtain only in exchange for their products. This exchange was everywhere originally bound by traditional principles of reciprocity and not, as Adam Smith supposed in making barter the origin of the division of labour, based upon trade for gain (Polanyi, 1946, p. 50). All practical crafts were learnt by imitation within the family, where trades were passed down from father to son and mother to daughter. Even the mysteries of the written word were reserved for a specialist caste, for in Europe as in India priests learned an ancient sacred language that no one else knew. No one else needed to be literate because the priests were, and for a long time even most kings in early medieval Europe were illiterate because they did not need to read in order to rule.

Comparing the division of labour in such a society with that existing in an industrial society, Ernest Gellner in his remarkable book on the rise of nations and nationalism noted

> a subtle but profound and important qualitative difference in the division of labour . . . The difference is this: the major part of training in industrial society is generic training, not specifically connected with the highly specialised professional activity of the person in question, and preceding it. Industrial society may by most criteria be the most highly specialised society ever; but its educational system is unquestionably the least specialised, the most universally standardised that has ever existed. The same kind of training or education is given to all or most children and adolescents up to an astonishingly late age . . . The central fact – the pervasiveness and importance of generic, unspecialised training – is conjoined to highly specialised industrial society not as a paradox, but as something altogether fitting and necessary. The kind of specialisation found in industrial society rests precisely on a common foundation of unspecialised and standardised training . . . The assumption is that anyone who has completed the generic training common to the entire population can be re-trained for most other jobs without too much difficulty . . . There is also a minority of genuine specialists, people whose effective occupancy of their posts really

depends on very prolonged additional training, and who are not easily or at all replaceable by anyone not sharing their own particular educational background.
(Gellner, 1983, p. 27)

This description of the development of training, instructive though it is, somewhat ignores the separate development of education. Originating in the courtly tradition, 'general education' became what Friedrich Ebert, founder of the German SPD, called 'the vocational education of the ruling class' (quoted by the Institute for Public Policy Research, 1990, p. 1). Later, when mass schooling developed, 'vocational education' became, as Ebert added, 'the general education of the working class'. There were thus two traditions: 'The academic tradition stems essentially from the curriculum of the nineteenth century public schools designed to perpetuate an elite' and based upon the classics, while for the mass of the working population, elementary education when it came was 'designed to control rather than emancipate' (Whitty, 1983, p. 105). Beyond this, trade training, such as it was, developed from apprenticeships and its formal elements became relegated, until recently, to evening classes and day-release in colleges of further education.

Education after the Renaissance began for the first time to present itself as something other than a training or apprenticeship of a particular type. That this separation of the general from the particular, privileging the mental over the physical, should occur then may appear surprising, since the predominant ideal of 'Renaissance man' is that these masculine heroes combined sublime art and inventive practicality in the manner of a Leonardo. However, criticism of the Renaissance can go too far towards a new pre-Raphaelitism. For it can be argued, as by Zuboff, that the Western separation of body from mind in manual and mental work originated not in the Renaissance but in what she describes as the medieval 'loathing' for manual labour. This, she says, was drawn from three traditions: '(1) The Greco-Roman legacy that associated labor with slavery, (2) the barbarian heritage that disdained those who worked the land and extolled the warrior who gained his livelihood in bloody booty, (3) Judeo-Christian theology that admired contemplation over action' (Zuboff, 1988, p. 25). However, the Renaissance brought with it a revival of classical learning, especially neo-Platonism, which elevated abstract reasoning over mundane toil undertaken by slaves. It was this learning that, despite its supposedly universal appeal, created the ideal of both the inspired artist/genius and the educated gentleman. 'The idea that there was an insuperable barrier between the worker and the artist (in the modern sense of the word) only appeared with the Renaissance and was expressed at that time by intellectuals who judged, classified and stratified manual work of which they had no experience' (Gimpel, 1983, p. 67). Thus, despite the invention of printing, 'the introduction of the classics separated the educated man from the people for several centuries' (Gimpel, 1983, p. 38). Similarly Edward Lucie-Smith, in *The Story of Craft* (1981), wrote, 'The two things which did the most to change the nature of medieval society, and with it the character of medieval craft attitudes, were printing, revolutionised by the introduction of moveable type, and the invention of the mechanical clock' (p. 138). For 'All craft processes took on a different complexion as soon as they began to be costed according to the precise amount of time they consumed' (p. 142). Simultaneously, printed books and plans enabled conception to be separated from execution. Michelangelo, for example, reasserted Plato's description of the architect in *The Republic* as a man who 'is not himself a workman, but a director of workmen contributing theoretical knowledge not practical craftsmanship' (Coulton, 1977, p. 15).

In fact, most paradoxically, printing, which potentially for the first time put literacy within the reach of everyone, at the same time created the basis for new distinctions based upon education in the codes of grammar, spelling and punctuation then being formalized for the first time. This continues to be the case today, for every state school teacher will agree with Martell, who wrote, 'As you move down the socio-economic class scale, kids read and write less well' (Martell, 1976, p. 107). Indeed, even in the age of the calculator and spell-checker, there continues to be insistence upon spelling and elementary maths as a means of differentiating between pupils. This is emphasized by the testing system imposed upon schools by the 1988 Education Reform Act.

Despite this repeated stress upon the traditional three Rs, at the beginning of the nineteenth century it was with surprisingly low rates of literacy that Britain succeeded as the first country to pioneer industrial revolution. Yet strangely the classical ideal lived longer in Britain than elsewhere. By the mid-nineteenth century English education was dominated by the classics to an extent that the historian Hugh Trevor-Roper (1973) found extraordinary: 'For surely it must strike any historian as odd that an industrial revolution, having triumphed at home, was carried over the whole world by the elite of society bred up on the literature of a city state and an empire whose slave-owning ruling class regarded industry and commerce as essentially vulgar.' Yet the industrial revolution had happened in Britain without the benefits of universal education and systematic training. In part this was because, as Hobsbawm (1969, p. 60) pointed out, 'The early industrial revolution was technically rather primitive.' It was not until what Landes (1972, p. 151) described as 'the exhaustion of the technological possibilities of the industrial revolution' by the end of the nineteenth century that scientific research began to contribute directly to production processes, and so general scientific education became important. In fact, as Green (1990) demonstrated, England lagged far behind other Western countries in this respect and arguably still does. However, in countries like Prussia and France, which introduced compulsory universal elementary education literally a century before England, Green showed that the establishment of education systems had less to do with preparation for the universal literacy supposedly necessary for industrial success and more to do with ensuring the adherence of citizens to a national state that in England was already secure. When education reform did come to England it was piecemeal and diverse, as continues to be the case. This is of course both a strength and a weakness but it contributes to and arose from the national predilection for 'muddling through', combined with distrust of Continental rationalizations and sweeping, philosophical totalizations. These deep-seated cultural characteristics were confirmed, and in part created, by the unique historical experience of pioneering industrial revolution.

That revolution of course had disastrous effects upon the traditional skills of handicrafts that mass production has today relegated to a specialized market in arts and crafts. The impression of a general deskilling is conveyed by Adam Smith's celebrated account in *The Wealth of Nations* of pin-making:

> One man draws out the wire, another straights it, a third cuts it, a fourth points it, a fifth grinds it at the top for receiving the head; to make the head requires three distinct operations; to put it on is a peculiar business, to whiten the pins is another; it is even a trade by itself to put them into the paper; and the important business of making a pin is, in this manner, divided into about eighteen distinct operations, which, in some manufactories, are all performed by distinct hands . . . Each person . . . might be considered as making four

thousand eight hundred pins a day. But if they had all wrought separately and independently . . . they certainly could not each of them have made twenty.
(Smith, 1774, pp. 6-7)

Despite the economic advantages, Smith saw the damage being done to the workers, for 'The man whose life is spent in performing a few simple operations . . . has no occasion to exert his understanding . . . He naturally loses, therefore, the habit of such exertion, and generally becomes as stupid and ignorant as it is possible for a human creature to become' (Smith, 1776, p. 267).

Marx, who developed Smith's argument, also emphasized the physical degradation and mental alienation of the workers by their subjection to machinery they neither owned nor controlled. Optimistically, he saw a way out of the situation and in *Capital* (Marx, 1971, p. 493) approvingly quotes a letter from a French printer who had travelled to California in search of employment:

> I never could have believed, that I was capable of working at the various occupations I was employed on in California. I was firmly convinced that I was fit for nothing but letter-press printing . . . Once in the midst of this world of adventurers, who change their occupation as often as they do their shirt, egad, I did as the others. As mining did not turn out remunerative enough, I left it for the town, where in succession I became typographer, slater, plumber, &c. In consequence of thus finding out that I am fit for any sort of work, I feel less of a mollusk and more of a man.

This letter is quoted in a footnote to *Capital* in which Marx describes the inherently revolutionary and restless nature of 'Modern Industry', which 'never looks upon and treats the existing form of a process as final' but 'is continually causing changes not only in the technical base of production, but also in the functions of the labourer, and in the social combinations of the labour process . . . It thereby also revolutionises the division of labour within the society, and incessantly launches masses of capital and working people from one branch of production to another.' This results in 'a social anarchy which turns every economical progress into a social calamity'. However, this is only the 'negative side', for 'Modern Industry . . . compels society . . . to replace the detail worker of today, crippled by life-long repetition of one and the same trivial operation, and thus reduced to a mere fragment of a man, by the fully developed individual, fit for a variety of labours, ready to face any change in production, and to whom the different social functions he performs, are but so many modes of giving free scope to his own natural and acquired powers.' These were the grounds on which Marx looked forward to the communist millennium in which the divisions between specialized occupations by hand and by brain, between men and women, and in town and countryside would be overcome by the development of machinery.

It was ironic that when the Russian revolution proclaimed the first workers' state it was its leader, Lenin, who, to develop industry as rapidly as possible in the terrible conditions following war and civil war, urged the adoption of Taylorist methods copied from the United States. There, in 1899, Frederick Taylor had systematically applied work study to get a Dutchman named Schmidt to carry forty-seven instead of twelve and a half tons of pig iron a day in a barrow. Schmidt, Taylor considered, was an ideal candidate on whom to pilot work study, for he was 'so stupid and so phlegmatic that he more nearly resembles in his mental make-up the ox than any other type' (Taylor, 1947, p. 59). The same 'scientific' management could also be applied to the burgeoning offices where Taylor's principle required all organization and control to be located in the hands of management, because, just as Gilbreth had defined 'therbligs' as the elementary physical movements to be timed and optimized, Clay defined 'yalcs' as 'mental therbligs' to be treated similarly (see Cooley, 1975). Braverman (1974) also predicted a universal degradation of work following from the application of Taylorist methods developed on the automated shop-floor to the computerized office. Whether this was the effect of the latest applications of new technology became the subject of a prolonged and academic 'labour process debate'.

NEW TECHNOLOGIES, NEW SKILLS

Mass production was multiplied in its effects by Henry Ford's introduction of the assembly line (modelled, incidentally, on the systematic disassembly of pigs in an abattoir). The deskilling effect of increasing capital investment in machinery to save labour costs and to control growing armies of labour regimented together in ever-larger factories was checked only by the more or less organized reaction of the workers and the development of technology itself under conditions of competition between rival employers. Trade unions and professional associations could succeed in imposing some control over the work processes to which their members were subject. Like the medieval guilds before they degenerated into self-serving oligarchies, combinations could maintain the mysteries of their craft, originally imparted by rituals handed down from an ancient age-graded past. Even the new general unions at the end of the nineteenth century asserted some control over their situation, whatever the degree of skill involved in their trade, not only by collectively withholding their labour but also by controlling entry to employment, for example in docking. With regard to professional associations,

> A strong profession requires a real technical skill that produces demonstrable results and can be taught. Only thus can the skill be monopolized by controlling who will be trained. The skill must be difficult enough to require training and reliable enough to produce results. But it cannot be too reliable, for the outsiders can judge work by its results and control its practitioners by their judgments. The ideal profession has a skill that occupies a mid-point in a continuum between complete predictability and complete unpredictability of results.
> (Collins, 1979, pp. 132–3)

For some time medicine has occupied this situation, combining in the paradoxical world of the modern hospital 'professional expertise, ultra-high technology and complete uncertainty' (Ballard, 1991, p. 247). The Manpower Services Commission (1985, p. 7) cited a case study of computer medical diagnosis in which, 'While the new system could displace personal medical skill, this role is not usually delegated to junior staff or to patients on a self-administration basis, although both methods are technically feasible.' This was because 'The archetypal professions such as medicine and law have been particularly successful in defending the status and standing of their practices against technological encroachment.' However, where occupational groups are not so strongly organized, as technology develops to produce greater certainty of results, trades and professions may be more or less deskilled. Their assertion of skill is then more a defensive means of control than anything else and their bluff may be called when their employers are strong enough to do so. This was the case in the early 1980s with printing even though the printers' unions had managed to delay the introduction of new technology for many years. At the same time new trade and professional associations can develop upon the basis of new, though usually fewer and more uncertain, operations using more capital-intensive and elaborate technology.

This constant social struggle over the definition of skill does not mean that skill is always and everywhere a purely social construction, as some feminist writers have claimed in pointing to arbitrary divisions between the supposed skills used in 'men's and women's work' (e.g. Cockburn, 1983, 1986). Phillips and Taylor (1980) gave one of many examples where the work being undertaken by women, in their case in a cardboard box factory, was objectively harder physically and required greater dexterity, hand–eye coordination, mental effort, etc. than the operation of new machines by men, which preserved their status as 'skilled' workers over 'unskilled' women. As Brady (1984) summarized, 'It would appear that the extent to which an occupation is "deskilled" bears some relationship to the "power" of the members of the occupation. Thus it is unlikely that doctors' or senior design engineers' work will be significantly deskilled by the use of automatic diagnostic systems whereas clerks', craftsmen's, or technicians' skills may well be – depending on management policy.' There is thus, as Gallie noted,

> little consensus between analysts about what constitutes skill or how it can be measured . . . The very complexity of the task of defining skill makes it implausible that skill classifications in industry reflect in an unproblematic way some objective hierarchy. Rather, they are likely to be the product of a continuous negotiation between employers and employees, in which both relative power resources and prevalent cultural beliefs will influence the grading structure.
>
> (Gallie, 1988, pp. 7–8)

As traditionally defined in British manufacturing industry, within the basic distinction between manual, blue-collar, wage workers and non-manual, white-collar, salaried staff, skill levels were the basis for wage rates for hourly paid workers. However inadequately defined, skilled, semi-skilled and unskilled were recognized as categories in the wages structures of most industries and, to an extent, in the class structure of society.

> Although it is impossible to define these categories [skilled, semi-skilled and unskilled] with any degree of precision, the terms are commonly used and understood throughout industry. It is generally accepted that a skilled worker is a craftsman whose training has been spread over several years and is formally recognised outside an individual firm, a semi-skilled worker is one who, during a limited period of training, usually between two and twelve weeks, has acquired the manual dexterity or mechanical knowledge needed for his immediate job, and an unskilled worker is one whose job requires no formal training of any kind.
>
> (Woodward, 1965, pp. 28–9)

These traditional distinctions have broken down with the application of new technology and especially information technology to industrial processes. As Burgess (1986, p. 123) wrote,

> The existing classifications of occupations as craftsmen, technicians, technologists and engineers already seem inappropriate in the light of the changes wrought by new technology. The enlargement of some jobs in clerical and administrative occupations to include other skills, such as social skills needed for selling and counselling, means that existing classifications fail to categorise new jobs properly.

The arbitrariness of traditional divisions is further apparent when it is considered that there is no job that is totally unskilled or that does not have a knack that it takes some practice to acquire. The BBC World Service news (16 May 1987) relayed an item concerning two cleaners in Scotland who came to blows over a dispute about how to mop a floor correctly. Before the incident that brought them to court, these two women, who worked together, had not spoken for the past seven years owing to their fundamental disagreement upon this matter of technique! (see also Kusterer, 1978). In fact, the division between formally trained skilled workers and the informally assimilated unskilled is one that is often not based on the task in hand but imposed upon it for the convenience of management. Management does not always designate down, however; for instance, Finn (1984) recorded that there was an increasing tendency for jobs described as 'casual' to be redesignated 'semi-skilled' by the addition of 'training programmes' as a form of work discipline. Such redesignations can operate quite arbitrarily up or down the labour hierarchy independently of what workers actually do.

This arbitrariness does *not* mean that skill is a category devoid of any real content, even if that content is undefinable, save by the criterion of Pye's uncertainty principle. There is always a triangular definition of skill that comprises not only the person performing the task and the social estimation of the skill involved in it but also the task itself. As well as Pye's uncertainty principle, further criteria that could be applied to the estimation of skill are those of repeatability (i.e. it was not just luck that enabled successful performance of the task first time round) and replaceability (i.e. as has been alluded to in the case of management functions, the task could not just as certainly be completed by someone possessing only the skills of an accomplished actor). An example of the latter was cited by Naftulin *et al.* (1973), who got an actor to deliver a lecture 'charismatically and nonsubstantively on a topic about which he knew nothing' to prove that 'even experienced educators participating in a new learning experience can be seduced into feeling satisfied that they have learnt despite irrelevant, conflicting, and meaningless content conveyed by the lecturer'.

Two further qualifications could also be considered with relation to real or supposed skills. One is the obvious one that not every task that is risky is also skilled; for example, gambling that depends on the chance cast of the die or turn of the wheel (though some gamblers consider that they are skilful at these activities). The other is that a simple task, or a task that has already been learnt and can be accomplished satisfactorily, may be rendered difficult or impossible by decomposition into its constituent elements. Examples of this are 'stage fright' or 'exam nerves', when, although one has learnt the entire speech, or knows the answer to the question, one is paralysed by inability to proceed to the next step. Instead of being self-conscious, it is only by directing conscious attention forward to the whole activity in which you are involved that the lost element finds its place in the total ensemble. Arguably, some enthusiasts for skills teaching by means of reductive flow charts or by behaviouristic approaches to deconstructing complex wholes into their individual parts succeed in making learning more difficult than it need be by these means. The same could be said of purely phonic approaches to the teaching of reading. Even where such methods are successful, e.g. in teaching typing, the directing of attention back to skills that have been 'taken for granted' in learning destroys the knack of coordinating them. The same effect can also be attained by medication that alters attention spans.

With these necessary clarifications, a typology can be constructed to apply to the tasks involved in different occupations and the training for them, in order to determine what is happening to the skills involved as new technology is applied to them. Thus, *enskilling* extends and develops existing skills within a given specialization, so that the ability to handle uncertainty is increased within that limited area. For example, craft-workers refine their trade by constant practice. *Multiskilling* retains existing skills while combining them with new skills in other areas. Thus the ability to handle uncertainty is increased by extension to a wider range of activities. For example, in flexible manufacturing an overall knowledge and ability to operate anywhere in the complete process is known as 'systems competence'. *Reskilling* means learning new skills in place of old so that the ability to handle the same level of uncertainty is retained but applied to a new specialization. For example, a printer becomes a carpenter, though how much the skills learnt for one activity are transferable to another depends on the similarity of the tasks and upon the identity of approach to them – how you think about them and how much similar general habits of mind apply to each case. It can be noted that information technology, which integrates so many different activities, tends towards making formerly discrete tasks increasingly identical. This does not necessarily lead to deskilling, for, as with other types of automation, 'Those who want to substitute human labor with machines must first arrange the job so that it can be done in a machine-like way; that is where so-called deskilling comes in' (Collins, 1989, p. 221). *Deskilling* means that the skills that would formerly have been acquired, through either study in a discipline or apprenticeship to a trade or profession, are lost. The range of uncertainty that could be handled is thus reduced and certainty of result is increased over a number of formerly discrete areas to gain the 'core skills' necessary for semi-skilled working instead of specialized craft work. This was noticeable in the shipbuilding industry, for example, when employers demanded an end to 'restrictive practices' and 'demarcations' between workers willing to move 'flexibly' between tasks and use new technology to perform them severally.

Enskilling, multiskilling, reskilling and deskilling can all happen simultaneously to individuals within one employment and to the workforce as a whole as technology changes. This has made it difficult to describe the overall effect of the exponentially rapid introduction of new technology, and especially integrative information technology, since the 1970s. As Hirschhorn (1986, p. 1) wrote, 'We are still mesmerized by the nineteenth century image of technology: mechanics and engineers together creating machines and machine systems that operate as if under immutable natural laws with workers only tending the machine.' And although, as he also cautioned, 'like one drug that makes another powerful, a technology can potentiate latent cultural trends' (p. 4), it cannot be repeated often enough that 'Technology as a fundamental human activity is intimately related to all other human activities and thus is an integral, indisposable part of all human culture and is not, as one so often hears, an alien inhuman force unleashed upon mankind by some external agent' (Mayr, 1986, p. xv).

It is not only analysts who are so 'mesmerized' by the past, but also the employers and managers who first introduced information technology in the same way that they had previously used other machinery to automate industrial processes. This was accompanied by labour shedding, leading to deskilling and semi-skilled working. However, as Zuboff (1988) pointed out, 'information technology supersedes the traditional logic of automation' because IT is 'characterised by a fundamental duality that has not yet been fully appreciated'. IT, as she put it, 'informates as well as automates'.

> As long as the technology is treated narrowly in its automating function, it perpetuates the logic of the industrial machine that, over the course of this century, has made it possible to rationalise work while decreasing the dependence on human skills. However, when the technology also informates the processes to which it is applied, it increases the explicit information content of tasks and sets in motion a series of dynamics that will ultimately reconfigure the nature of work and the social relationships that organise productive activity.
> (Zuboff, 1988, pp. 9–11)

Zuboff's book illustrated in fascinating detail this effect of the introduction of 'smart machines' into a variety of working environments, to the extent even of describing how process workers removed from contact with the vats in which they previously stirred boiling pulp, until they 'felt' that it was ready to be poured out, now view the whole papermaking process on screen but attempt to 'stab at' the screens in the same way they previously stirred the vats. (This exercise of tacit knowledge may yet be directly retained by the use of keyboardless computers, in which mice and gloves may be used to 'pull down' information and perform operations upon it inside an artificial 'cyberspace'.)

It can be argued that Braverman's (1974) description of 'the degradation of work' came too soon to appreciate the capacity of computers not only to automate and deskill industrial and office work, with resultant labour shedding, but also to generate information potentially accessible by all employees and not just their managers. As the information generated by the technology became more widely accessible, some reskilling and even enskilling occurred among the core of remaining employees and their managers – positions rendered increasingly similar and overlapping. Similarly, 'Operating personnel are provided with technical calculations and economic data, conventionally only available to technical staff' (Hirschhorn, 1986, p. 2). At the same time, flexibility is also increased by shorter production runs for personally customized commodities so that, with miniaturized equipment, there is a reversal of the previously seemingly inevitable tendency towards larger and larger aggregations of workers and machinery in factory production, at least in the developed countries. As well as devolving production to smaller 'teams' , the 'flexible firm' divests itself of many of its previously integrated functions and with the latest communications can coordinate its supply, production and assembly across countries and continents. 'At the extreme the core of an organization need contain no more than a design function, a quality control function, a costing and estimating function and a marketing function, as well as some coordinating management' (Handy, 1984, p. 80).

'Flexible' organization is not restricted to the private sector but extends to public services. Following the recommendations of the 1988 Ibbs Report, the civil service is moving towards the creation of autonomous executive agencies with delegated responsibilities for carrying out specific policy functions. This 'government by quango', as Ainley and Corney (1990, p. 136) called it, or 'franchise model of state-induced enterprise' (Wallace and Chandler, 1989), leads to the state as holding company subcontracting to agencies that can be expanded and disbanded to task. It centralizes control while dispersing responsibility; problems are privatized as democratic accountability is lost. Such a 'contract culture', as it is now widely known, was encouraged by the entrepreneurial spirit unleashed upon public services in the 1980s by successive Conservative governments. Their version of *perestroika* created for the 1990s a new mixed economy that would blur the distinction between the privatized state sector and the state-subsidized private sector (see Chapter 5).

There is considerable debate as to how far this 'flexible', core–periphery model of industrial and commercial organization within and without the state sector has developed in Britain. It appears limited compared with its home base in Japan, while how far such a reorganization represents a new 'post-Fordist' stage of industrial organization is another source of debate. This discussion is linked to that about how far services have taken over from manufacturing in developed economies. Much service work, involving contact with customers as well as routine and often casual employment, erodes the old divisions between manual and mental labour and the conventional distinctions between 'men's' and 'women's' work. The traditional divisions between skilled, semi-skilled and unskilled manual labour are also lost. The new model of employment implies a new distribution between a regularly employed, multiskilled minority and an irregularly employed, deskilled majority to be used and discarded as economic demand dictates. The term 'skill' could have changed its meaning again from a technical to a behavioural description. As Morgan and Sayer (1988) noted in their study of 'sunrise' industries using Japanese corporate structures, this new meaning of skill 'is rarely defined, but it seems to refer not so much to the technical qualifications of employees but to their qualities as "good company employees" in terms of attendance, flexibility, responsibility, discipline, identification with the company and, crucially, work-rate and quality . . . On this concept, "shortage of skills" often means the lack of workers who have fully adjusted to corporate standards' (p. 167).

The decision on whether there is an overall deskilling, enskilling or bifurcation between new multiskilled and un/semi-skilled in production and services is complicated further by consideration of changing patterns of consumption. On the one hand, for those who can afford them, increasingly sophisticated consumer durables perform more and more sophisticated tasks. Equipment that was only a short time ago restricted to specialists is now purchasable in every high street: computers, robots, videocameras and recorders, synthesizers, hi-fi, CB radio, mixing and recording studios, do-it-yourself tools and all the gadgetry of kitchen, garage and garden. Often these consumables are sold only in order to be consumed in use and so cannot be easily repaired, but there is in consumption a levelling up of skills across a range of activities, including those in which customers are increasingly expected to serve themselves. Skills are required not only for work but also in order to benefit from leisure activities. On the other hand, much consumption is increasingly passive and, as traditional communities decay, knowledge and skills that were previously acquired informally become the business of new service workers who range from professional 'experts' of various sorts to new-style domestic servants. Just surviving independently in modern society depends on much more than functional numeracy, literacy and the habits of punctuality and regularity with which mass schooling during the industrial era attempted to equip the future workforce. Similarly, much employment now requires more than the 'general mechanical intelligence' that the Crowther Report on 15 to 18 education (HMSO, 1959) assumed was necessary for all citizens. Many occupations require at least keyboard familiarity with computers, and modern European languages are increasingly in demand.

For optimists, these increasing demands being made upon the new generations of the workforce are reason to believe that at last the old divisions between white and blue collar, office and shop-floor, those who decide and those who do, can be overcome as the country moves towards a high-skill economy requiring the extension to all of lifelong education, training and retraining combined in a mass system of universal higher education. For pessimists, the collapse of industry into a low-skill, service economy merely replaces the old divisions of labour and class with a new core–periphery pattern of employment in which power and the information to make decisions rest with a narrowing elite of managers. To decide which of these two scenarios is most possible and likely it is necessary to move from a consideration of skill to an examination of class.

Chapter 3

What Has Happened to Social Class?

Any reference to class distinctions is a Marxist concept.
(Margaret Thatcher, interview in *Vanity Fair*, June 1991)

MARX ON THE MIDDLE CLASS

Mrs Thatcher was right of course, even though historians before Marx had analysed history in terms of a struggle between classes. It was the importance Marx gave to that struggle as the engine of history, together with the recognition he and Engels insisted upon of the necessity, if not the inevitability, of an eventual rule by the majority, working class, that stamps the class concept with the brand of its maker. In its original form it was not a sociological description of events but a political analysis intended to guide and assess action upon them. It derived all social phenomena, including individual consciousness, from a determination of the ruling class in the state, together with its relations of power over the subordinate classes variously struggling against or in alliance with it. Power was expressed as ownership or control over property, be that slaves, land or money. As long as it was not applied dogmatically, Marx's concept of class provided a subtle and flexible means of analysing and describing more than contemporary society. It afforded a firm basis upon which to construct a plan of the whole social system and to plot the course of history. Hence the alarm, heart-searching and even panic when events appear to move reality beyond reach of the paradigm as classes change their form or even appear no longer to exist. As K. Polanyi (1946, p. 154) asked, 'Given a definite structure of society, the class theory works; but what if that structure itself undergoes a change?'

Given the continuing debate over the validity of the concept, it is remarkable that the original notions of the founders of class analysis are widely misconceived. It may be tedious to return to the original texts to find how Marx and Engels defined social class, partly because they did so in different ways and for different purposes but mainly because they wrote so much that, as with the Bible or any other holy work, anyone can find in their many tomes something to prove his or her own contention. It is, however, necessary to read Marx in view of the misconceptions that exist, particularly to see how fluid, provisional and subject to constant revision were the formulations of the founders of scientific socialism. This is clearly apparent in their pronouncements upon the middle class, which are far removed from the stereotyped picture of a simple, two-class Marxist schema, but in which confusion is confounded by a problem of the English language.

The widely held, simple and rather mechanical view of the Marxist notion of class derives from *The Communist Manifesto*. This best-known of all the works of Marx and Engels was not an attempt at a scientific description of society. It was rather a call to action, which as a political document contained necessary simplifications and as revolutionary poetry sought to inspire a vision of history without qualifying each point of the grand narrative. In this epic vision, 'the history of all hitherto existing societies' is contained in the ceaseless struggle between two main antagonistic classes to seize, retain or recapture power over the state. Of course, the idea that a struggle of opposites determined the development not just of state societies, but of everything in existence, came from Marx's reading of Hegel. It was given an extension that tended towards the mechanical by Engels's later attempt to justify its validity with reference to the latest discoveries of Victorian science. Thus for Engels, atoms, for example, also existed in constant tension between (in their case) the opposite charges of electron and proton. Similarly, a struggle between polar opposites drove societies along the cosmic sweep of the meta-narrative from the prehistory of primitive communism towards the return to communism at a higher stage. Then 'real history' would begin under conscious human control and other contradictions would determine the development of international, classless, stateless society. In this context, again following Hegel, feudal lord and peasant succeeded ancient master and slave before in turn giving way to capitalist and worker. The ruling class in each stage sows the seeds of its own destruction by creating the social opposite that overthrows it. So, under feudalism, the landowning class living from the direct appropriation of the produce of the peasantry could not prevent the development of technology and trade that permitted the growth of a middle class, intermediate between it and the peasants.

This is where the problem of language comes in. In an effort to found a new science of history, as rigorous in the specification of its general laws as Darwin's similar formulation of the principle of evolution to explain the course of natural history, Marx and Engels tried to agree a common definition of scientific terms. This was all the more necessary because the social democratic movement, as the communists were then called, was attempting to put theory into practice by organizing itself in various different countries. Like other scientists, they borrowed from the still current international language of Latin, from which comes 'proletariat'. But the French words 'bourgeoisie' and 'petit bourgeoisie' had already gained a shared international understanding in the French revolution, which was then the prototype of revolutionary change. The bourgeoisie that had emerged victorious from this social upheaval was plainly understood in France and elsewhere as the capitalist class of bankers, financiers and industrialists who had disappropriated the feudal aristocracy. But this bourgeois class was previously in the middle between the aristocracy and the peasantry. In the new situation the bourgeoisie were the new rulers of the new society created by industrialization and revolution, and the peasantry was being transformed into a proletariat of free labourers. The people who are now called 'middle class', intermediate between the capitalist ruling class and the proletariat it employed, Marx called petit bourgeois, at least in a general if not a narrow sense (see pp. 74-5). This is the source of the first confusion, further confounded in Britain by the alliance of industrial capitalists with the urban professional and clerical 'middling orders', who saw themselves as a 'middle class' united against the old (but no longer feudal) aristocracy of land and money above them and the propertyless working class below them.

This was not Marx's 'scientific analysis'. He shared his scheme with the bourgeois economists he criticized, Smith and Ricardo. The only difference between them, as far as description of society in class terms was concerned, was that Marx did not treat rent and interest separately as sources of income for two different classes of landowners and capitalists but predicted (correctly) that these two groups would in Britain join together with the amalgamation of industrial capitalists and landed aristocrats. This left two main classes as the model for pure capitalism as an ideal type, although not in reality.

The capitalist ruling class was very small – roughly, as Marx said, 'the top ten thousand' in any given capitalist country. It was estimated by Scott as 43,500 in Britain in 1991, which equals the 0.1 per cent of the adult population who own or otherwise control giant business enterprises, large landed estates and massive share portfolios, separate from but intermingled with the political elite who exercise power on its behalf and distinguished again from smaller capitalists, as well as from managers and supervisors in the private and also in the state sector. So, for Marx, 'The real constitution of society in no way simply consists of the working class and the industrial capitalists.' And again, in *Theories of Surplus Value*, Marx referred to 'the constantly growing number of the middle classes, those who stand between the workman on the one hand and the capitalist and landlord on the other'. Even in Britain, where for Marx 'modern society is indisputably developed most highly and classically in its economic structure . . . the stratification of classes does not appear in its pure form . . . Middle and transitional stages obliterate even here all definite boundaries.' In America, although Marx thought classes could be said to exist, he believed that 'they have not yet become fixed but continually change and interchange their elements in constant flux' (quoted in Goldthorpe, 1980, p. 7). Elsewhere, for example in the famous *Eighteenth Brumaire of Louis Napoleon*, Marx lists the 'third persons' who exist between the two principal social antagonists of workers and capitalists. These include left-overs from feudalism, like small farmers and handicraftsmen, priests, shopkeepers, lawyers, state officials, professors, artists, teachers, doctors and soldiers 'who exist on the basis of capitalist production but do not participate in it', and merchants, middlemen, speculators, commercial agents, as well as managers, foremen and other officials who 'command in the name of capital', so that 'the governing caste . . . is by no means identical with the ruling class' (quoted in Hall, 1977, p. 49). There is also in the *Brumaire* a lumpenproletariat below the proletariat, almost as various in its peculiar occupations as those lists of beggars and street hawkers compiled by contemporary Victorian investigators like Booth and Mayhew, Jack London's (1903) 'people of the abyss'.

Such diversity of description is a long way from the crude stereotype of two classes. However, what pushes the complex reality in that simplified direction is the well-known tendency towards 'proletarianization' of the intermediate elements, numerous though they may be. In times of crisis, as Marx said, all these third persons 'find themselves on the pavements'. And crises, as Marx showed, were endemic to the system of unregulated competition between independent capitalists. With each slump in the trade cycle, however, 'one capitalist drives out many' as the smaller capitals, unable to undercut their rivals or to hang on to their stockpiled goods until the next boom, go out of business. The free market thus tends inexorably towards monopoly, a tendency only partially offset by the emergence of new capitals associated with new markets for the products of new technologies. What is more, the merging of industrial with banked capital, which Marx predicted but did not live to see, was taken by Engels and later by Lenin, following Hobson and Hilferding, as marking the transition to a new and, Lenin thought, 'final' stage of capitalism, imperialism.

'Imperialism', Lenin wrote in his book of that name, 'somewhat changes the situation. A privileged upper stratum of the proletariat in the imperialist countries lives partly at the expense of the hundreds of millions in the undeveloped countries.' This is the orthodox Marxist explanation for why Marx's prophecy of proletarianization of the intermediate strata was not fulfilled in the polarization of society between a minority of monopoly capitalists and the vast mass of people with no property. It is the source of Engels's repeatedly expressed disillusion with the English working class, which, he wrote in his letters, 'is more bourgeois than the bourgeoisie' and 'gaily shares in the feast of England's monopoly of the world market and the colonies', so that in England 'no real labour movement exists' but only 'a bourgeois labour party'. Engels viewed with disgust 'the bourgeois "respectability" which has grown deep into the bones of the workers', so that a 'labour aristocracy' of skilled workers separated itself off from the mass of the unskilled. This antagonism between the English working class, which identified with its masters against inferior foreigners, was, Engels had long considered, the 'secret' of the continued command of the English ruling class.

According to Lenin, the 'super-profits' generated by imperialism enabled the bourgeoisie (in the sense of the capitalist ruling class) to distribute enough wealth to sustain a social bloc in support of its rule. This included not only the mass of the non-manual middle class, proliferating into professionalism at its top end and into clerical administration in the burgeoning bureaucracy of empire at the bottom, but also the upper, respectable, skilled strata of the manual working class. Thus by the end of the nineteenth century, as Landes said, precisely the opposite to Marx's prediction had occurred: 'Instead of polarising society into bourgeois minority and an almost all-embracing proletariat, the Industrial Revolution produced a heterogeneous bourgeoisie whose multitudinous shadings of income, origin, education, and way of life are overridden by a common resistance to inclusion in, or confusion with, the working classes, and by an unquenchable social ambition' (Landes, 1972, p. 9). In this sense, the bourgeoisie, or more generally bourgeois society, includes practically everybody save the unrespectable and unwashed; 'that section of the public that has no hope or ambition of becoming thrusting executives', as one of William Rees-Mogg's editorials in *The Times* (17 September 1975) once memorably put it, or those whom Mrs Thatcher repeatedly placed beyond the pale of 'responsible public opinion'. This hierarchy of infinite gradations and complexity can appear caste-like, even down to its army of untouchable street people, or semi-feudal, like such a social anachronism as the British monarchy (Nairn, 1988). Yet the stability of the British social formation and allegiance to the crown that represents subjection to it can be explained by Britain's unique history, culminating in the century of its imperial dominance. 'It has', wrote Richard Johnson (1985, p. 227), 'succeeded in a way no other state in the world has done.' Even in its long decline during the twentieth century, 'this state was immune from revolution . . . it never tolerated notions of federalism . . . It even refused, uniquely, to subject its absolute sovereignty to a constitution.'

As for its rulers, those 'persons economically free and accustomed to responsibility from an early age', in a phrase from a governor of the BBC rivalling Rees-Mogg's for its elegant circumlocution (quoted in Marwick, 1980, p. 159), one alternative to an explanation of history in terms of social class is explanation in terms of elites. After examining large estates willed at decease, Rubinstein (1987) suggested that 'mid-Victorian Britain contained two middle classes', or, as Marxists would say, 'two bourgeoisies' or (more orthodoxly) 'two fractions of the bourgeoisie'. 'By far the larger and wealthier was based on commerce and London, the other on manufacturing and the north of England. Together with the landed elite, these contested for the benefits of wealth, status and power, and evolved separate means of social control. These separate elites replaced the unified eighteenth century world of "Old Corruption" and themselves merged, by a gradual process, into a single elite, finally formed in the period 1918-25' (Rubinstein, 1987, pp. 51-2). Only after the Second World War and the long boom following it, as imperial protection and the value of sterling were lost, was the division between City and industry again pulled apart by the rival attractions of continuing with financial speculation in subservience to the United States, or of trying to save what was left of indigenous manufacturing within the European Common Market. This was symptomatic of the other change in rulership that has occurred during Britain's imperial dotage, as increasing penetration of foreign capital - European, American and Japanese - has reduced the room for independent manoeuvre by the ruling elite. 'The slight shrinkage of the state sector in the Thatcher years has been paralleled by an increase in the extent of foreign ownership' (Scott, 1991, p. 80). However, this was after the trauma of depression and war had given way to a temporary consolidation of the class structure during the anomalous but prolonged prosperity and growth of the 1950s and 1960s.

THE WAY WE WERE

Thanks largely to the limitations of the reforms implemented by the Labour Party, Britain escaped the social upheaval of total war with its class system virtually intact. This is nowhere more clear than in the area of education. As the public arena in which the state touches most directly and regularly upon the lives of its citizens, the juncture, in classical terms, of state and civil society, state education has a more than symbolic significance. It represents the future of society itself in the values and information thought worthy of communication to future generations (Ainley, 1988, p. 3). Moreover, the 1944 Education Act passed by the national government but implemented by Labour after 1945 was an important component of the welfare state. This is still the most enduring creation of British Labourism and, as Blackwell and Seabrook (1985, p. 37) recalled, is 'the English working class's great existential protest against the way they were told life had to be'. However, as part of this great settlement or compromise after the war, Labour's leaders did not even attempt to establish a universal system of equal education with open access to all. Rather, they followed the recommendations of the 1943 Norwood Report in introducing what became known as the tripartite system of secondary modern, technical and grammar schools at the secondary level. The Norwood Report had divided the male school population into three inherently unequal groups for whom three different types of education were deemed appropriate. First, there were those 'interested in learning for its own sake'; they would be able to benefit from higher education and go on to the management and professional positions in post-war society.

Then there were those who, while not so able intellectually, were capable of applying knowledge practically: 'He often has an uncanny insight into the intricacies of mechanism whereas the subtleties of language construction are too delicate for him.' This did not mean that these boys could not talk, but they were presumed to be the future skilled workers for the reconstructed economy. Finally there were the below average, who were 'incapable of a long series of connected steps'. This did not mean that they could not walk, but they were assumed to be the unskilled workers of the future. 'Whether such groupings are distinct on strictly psychological grounds, whether they represent kinds of minds, whether the differences are differences in kind or in degree, these are questions which it is not necessary to pursue' (HMSO, 1943, p. 201).

Nevertheless, it did not escape notice at the time that this convenient trisection of male children into three levels of intelligence – the academic, the technical and the practical (or the men of gold, bronze and iron of Plato's *Republic*) – corresponded to the traditional divisions of labour into workers by brain and by hand, the latter being subdivided again into the skilled and the unskilled. Such a division was ridiculed for presuming 'that the Almighty has benevolently created three types of child in just those proportions which would gratify educational administrators' (Curtis, 1952, pp. 144–5). However, it was the traditional division of labour that had served British industry so well in the past and upon which it was assumed that industry would be rebuilt to secure continuing prosperity in the future. Similarly women, it was supposed, would return from the factories and fields to resume their peacetime role as wives and mothers to replenish the nation's stock. In any case, 'women's work' was considered separately from the real, breadwinning labour upon which family wages depended. The tripartite education system that emerged from this vision of the future workforce was never realized, however, owing to underfunding and undervaluation of the technical schools designed to produce the skilled workers of the future. As late as 1958, secondary technical schools still contained only 4 per cent of the secondary school population and did not exist in more than 40 per cent of local education authorities (Schilling, 1989, p. 49). So the 'tripartite system' that actually emerged was between the private (public), grammar and secondary modern schools, many of the last renamed comprehensives after 1965.

Although excoriated before the war by Labour's most persuasive advocate of equality as 'the hereditary curse upon English education' and a 'barbarity' (Tawney, 1931, pp. 142, 145), the independence of the public schools was preserved by the 1944 Act, subject only to their periodic inspection. The intention of Labour's education policy lay 'in the state providing educational opportunities of such wide variety, encouraging experiments so comprehensive in character, and planning and staffing its schools to provide such high standards of teaching and amenities that no parent, however rich or however snobbish, could gain any advantage either in prestige or social opportunity by paying £315 a year to maintain his son at Eton' (quoted in Green, 1948, p. 161). As 'Red Ellen' Wilkinson, Labour's first Minister of Education after the war, put it to the 1946 Party conference: 'Free milk will be provided in Hoxton and Shoreditch, Eton and Harrow. What more social equality could you have than that?' Of course, as the hereditary and financial advantages of the private schools continued to exert such an unfair influence in the competition with the state sector, they, and the academic establishments of the antique universities which sustained them through their examination and entrance procedures, came to be the prime target – at least in rhetoric – of further promised reform.

It was the state system, over which they could have some influence via the Labour Party and the National Union of Teachers, that continued to be the main practical preoccupation of educational reformers. It was assumed that with an increase in 'access' and 'opportunities' – the terms in which the problem of opening education to more working-class children was conceived – society would gradually become more egalitarian, dissolving antediluvian class divisions in a rising sea of affluence so that the working class could actually be educated out of existence. From its inception, therefore, the new sociology of education developing in the expanded teacher training colleges and departments was peculiarly concerned with analysis in terms of 'class chances' of the reformed education system. This was long before Marxism was accepted on equal terms as a competing school of thought in the plural society of academia, but when 'The word "class" ', as Tawney put it, was still 'fraught with unpleasing associations, so that to linger upon it is apt to be interpreted as the symptom of a perverted mind and a jaundiced spirit' (quoted in Marwick, 1980, p. 7). The most famous of these descriptions of educational access in class terms was Jackson and Marsden's 1962 classic, *Education and the Working Class*, an account of the struggles of eighty-eight working-class children in the grammar schools of a northern industrial town. Their conclusion was that 'The children who lasted the full grammar school course came from the upper strata of the working class' (p. 152), and although 'most of the 88 completed their education happily and successfully . . . they are now middle-class citizens' (p. 153), who had bidden farewell to the working class (Greenslade, 1976). The system was thus self-perpetuating.

In fact, in his follow-up study of streaming, Jackson considered that the tripartite separation between private, grammar and secondary modern schools reflected and perpetuated traditional divisions in English society: 'an older generation usually accepted that our grandparents' society (like its railway carriages) had its 1st, 2nd and 3rd class: upper, middle and lower. Our world combines this ironic echo. In school uniform the child learns of the teacher–prefect–pupil triad. In army uniform he meets the firmness of the officer–NCO–men structure. The BBC "naturally" postulates three audiences, Third–Home–Light' (Jackson, 1964, p. 135). Bateson considered what he called 'ternary systems', such as parents–nurse–child, king–ministers–people or monitors–leaders–fags (at private schools), followed by first-, second- and third-class degrees at university, to typify the English national character before the war (Bateson, 1978, p. 69). For Jackson:

> The values that associate early selection with defeat on the playing fields are real enough: many teachers and parents share them – and in the world between 1850 and 1950 they were extraordinarily effective. There was no economic point in raising large hopes through education, for society had not the resources to satisfy them. Early selection of the few allowed the governing elites to recruit a new stream of talent from lower middle class homes. Eleven plus and streaming clarified the problem. It was as objective as any such procedures. It worked.
>
> (Jackson, 1964, pp. 135, 141)

Today, in so far as the 1988 Education Reform Act has reintroduced selective testing for opted-out grammar schools and strengthened the private sector, it seeks a return to this ideal and clearly ordered world. This was certainly the intention of many of its sponsors, as is made clear even from such an unashamedly biased and adulatory account of them as Knight's *The Making of Tory Education Policy in Post-war Britain* (1990). For these grammar school Tory seekers after educational 'excellence', the vision of a simply stratified world had the additional attraction that in it they occupied the comfortable position in the middle between two extremes. Or, even more gratifyingly to their self-esteem, like Mr Bounderby, the self-made man in Dickens's *Hard Times*, who never tires of telling anyone who will listen to him how he was born in a ditch, they feel that they have risen by dint of their own efforts and talents. Educational selection confirmed their elevation from manual labour into the ranks of the non-manual middle class, whose prime distinguishing mark from the masses below them always was that they did not have to get their hands dirty. This picture of how it used to be has such persistence not only because of its simplicity but also because for such a long time that was precisely how it was. Furthermore, traditional class divisions continued to impress themselves with such salience because, as Roberts *et al.* (1977, p. 24) pointed out, urbanized Britain did not leave room for the differences between town and country that persisted elsewhere, and ethnic, national and religious differences in Britain were relatively insignificant, at least after the partial assimilation of the Irish influx during the nineteenth century, of the Eastern European Jews who arrived before the First World War and until more large-scale black and Asian immigration from 1948 to 1962.

In addition, the media and particularly the televisual image of working-class life in the cities of the English North has been assiduously cultivated by 'a generation of programme makers whose idea of the English working class stood still when they left it two and more decades ago; then, as they remember it, the population everywhere was predominantly white and lived in terraced housing' (Ainley, 1991, p. 58). Even to those at the bottom, the memory of a simple stratified world in which each knew his or her place has its attractions, especially as recalled through the romanticized imagery of advertising, or the timeless and fictitious community of 'Coronation Street'. (See also 'Nostalgia rules – hokey cokey?' in Hobbs (1990) for a sentimental Cockney re-creation of what one of his informants called 'the way things used to be before the niggers moved in'.) So celebrated, nostalgia for a lost and more simple past corresponds to the reality of the pattern of working-class life that Hobsbawm (1969, p. 164) recorded was established between 1870 and 1900, and

> which the writers, dramatists and TV producers of the 1950s thought of as 'traditional' . . . It was not 'traditional' then, but new. It came to be thought of as age-old and unchanging, because it ceased in fact to change very much until the major transformation of British life in the affluent 1950s . . . It was neither a very good nor a very rich life, but it was probably the first kind of life since the Industrial Revolution which provided a firm lodging for the British working class within industrial society.

The classical factory proletariat of manual labourers, divided into skilled and unskilled, respectable and rough, was thus created earlier in Britain and lasted longer than in any other country. There was not even a peasantry in Britain to pose the problems of relations between the two great manual labouring classes that dogged communist parties and governments in other countries. Work-based organization among this factory proletariat distinguished truly socialist parties and groups from the electorally oriented ward organization of the Labour Party. That the soviet power of the future would be based on the factory floor was unproblematically accepted by classical Marxism.

The English working class was not particularly accepting of the heroic and historic role in which it had been cast. The parochialism and defensiveness of the traditional English working class has been remarked upon by many writers, who often forget how much of such a culture and its practices were elaborated over a long period of time to make their position in society bearable. Those who were sympathetic to it, such as Richard Hoggart (1958) decrying the effects of a mass, Americanized culture upon the traditional uses of literacy, or Wilmott and Young (1957) discovering an urban village in Bethnal Green, described and so preserved in academic aspic this working-class community just at the moment of its dissolution.

BEYOND THE GREAT DIVIDE

The liberation in British social attitudes 'Between the end of the Chatterley ban/And the Beatles' first LP', as Larkin wrote in June 1967, was superficial in many respects for many people. However, 'the sixties' are celebrated for at last sweeping away the fuddy-duddy old world of what suddenly came to be seen as petty, hierarchical class distinction. Preserved by rationing and austerity after the war, the orderly ideal of the tripartite social system collapsed in the scandals and incompetence of the Tory old boys running a government that became a joke. Everywhere events appeared to move beyond the control of England's natural rulers. Abroad the pretence of a new Elizabethan age of empire had been exposed by the humiliation of Suez. At home the old world of cosy working-class terraces was literally demolished and redeveloped. Anarchy seemed loosed upon the world as popular culture appropriated trends in fashion and music that had first appeared in the working class. With some modest affluence youth became for the first time a state to be enjoyed and prolonged, not a transient phase to be endured. The real differences in clothing indicated by the old labels, blue and white collar, were lost as manual workers could no longer be identified away from their workplaces now that they drove to work like everyone else, no longer walking cap on head, lunchbox in hand. New appetites were excited by mass marketing that put on every high street what had previously been exclusive first to the wealthy and then to some of the old middle class: televisions, fashion, holidays abroad. Together with the new availability of the pill, all this appealed particularly to the young, so that, together with parental controls over future generations, traditional class affiliations were further weakened.

So much that was holy was profaned, but it was not forgotten, at least not by the likes of Mrs Thatcher and Mary Whitehouse, those nagging grandmothers to the nation. People like them could not forgive those they held responsible for undermining the foundations of what they had been brought up to believe in. As suggested, the 1988 Education Reform Act embodies only one effort to turn the clock back and re-create that respectful and clear-cut world by fostering reborn grammar schools with selectivity at all levels – 'opportunities to be unequal', as Mrs Thatcher put it. This fondness for the tripartite hierarchy that made Britain great sat oddly with later Conservative declarations of 'classlessness', but this is the source of the bitter nostalgia for the days before rock and roll.

In the 1960s, however, it was Labour that could claim to be the classless party. Characteristically, Harold Wilson offered something for everybody, for example in his promise to make the new comprehensive schools 'grammar schools for all'. For the Labour governments of 1964 and 1966 embraced an alliance with science, as former double-barrelled hereditary peer Anthony Wedgwood Benn, now plain Tony Benn, forged at MinTech a bright future in the white heat of new technology. Instead of a return to the glories of the past, the industrial modernization that was attempted would, it was claimed, demand higher skills from more workers as drudgery and hard labour were replaced by automation. Blue collars would give way to white-coated technicians. Science and art might then be united in the laboratories and offices of the gleaming factories of the future. As much education as possible for as many people as possible was to be supplied by progressive primary and comprehensive secondary schooling, as well as by new universities, some specializing in science and technology, and by polytechnics, which were modelled on a Soviet ideal of combining practical and theoretical study and which might become 'the people's universities' (Robinson, 1968).

Those who feared the irreparable loss of the old tripartite class world in the upheavals of the 1960s need not have worried, however. The expansion of higher education, for instance, failed to overcome the manual–mental divide as it catered mainly for middle-class youth, offering them a route to preferred non-manual employment in the growing service and state sectors. As the Robbins Report recorded, the percentage of students from working-class homes had actually decreased from 27 per cent in 1928 to 26 per cent in 1961. Meanwhile, the skills of manual workers were acquired in what remained of technical education in formal institutions, largely part-time and in night schools at further education colleges. In the 1960s, 40 per cent of boys leaving school at age sixteen or earlier gained apprenticeships. This proportion was halved by 1981 as the number of school-leavers entering manufacturing apprenticeships fell from a peak of 236,000 in 1968 to under 100,000 in 1982. The number of other trainees in manufacturing fell from 210,000 in 1968 to 90,000 in 1980 (Manpower Services Commission, 1982, para. 2.2). This decline in training was often blamed at the time upon young workers themselves, who were seen as unprepared any longer to put in the work and sustained effort to gain the old apprenticeship skills, and on their unions for demanding excessively high wages for them and for unskilled workers. The old division within the working class between skilled and unskilled, respectable and rough, was eroded but this did not affect the deeper divide between manual and mental labour for which the schools, grammar or secondary modern/comprehensive, continued to sort pupils at fourteen-plus. Following the tradition established in Victorian times of early leaving to work, most pupils in England and Wales quit school at fifteen (sixteen after 1972); not until the 1980s did this begin to change. Indeed, the terms 'school-leaver' and 'working class' were virtual synonyms. But as unemployment and deskilling laid waste Britain's industrial heartlands, changes in the whole way of life of the manual working class sapped the traditional, informal, cultural apprenticeship by which habitual skills and attitudes had been acquired previously.

In retrospect it becomes clear that the period of full employment from after the war until the 1973 oil crisis can be seen as an anomaly that had been mistaken at the time for permanent reality. In the 1944 White Paper *Employment Policy*, the government had for the first time accepted 'as one of their primary aims and responsibilities the maintenance of a high and stable level of employment' (Cmnd 6527). This commitment had been a part of the all-party support for the welfare state. Despite these wartime assurances, it was widely anticipated that a prolonged depression, like that into which the economy had plunged shortly after the First World War, would recur soon after the ending of the Second. The post-war recovery proved not merely temporary as that of 1918 had been, however, but persisted, though with much faltering, into the long boom of the 1950s and 1960s. Overall, unemployment averaged little more than 1.5 per cent until the end of the 1960s, exceeding the apparently wildly optimistic expectations of

Beveridge during the war, when he said that if unemployment could be kept down to 3 per cent the country would be doing very well. The regional unemployment that had characterized the 1930s persisted in rates of 2 and 3 per cent in the North and in Scotland, while in Northern Ireland unemployment has never been less than 7 per cent. When overall unemployment began to rise, passing the one million mark in August 1975, there was a reluctance to admit to the permanence of such high levels. Labour governments clung to the post-war commitment to full employment and to a belief in the inevitable upturn in the cycle to meet the traditional socialist demand from the unions for the right to work. It was the Thatcher government at the instigation of Sir Keith Joseph that abandoned this consensus and accepted that the change was not cyclical but structural and permanent. With unemployment rising to three million and over, by 1981 it had been widely accepted that, as Adrian Sinfield wrote at the time, 'The days of "full employment" are not only over; they are as much a part of social history, which we may regard with nostalgia or contempt according to taste, as hoolahoops and spats' (Sinfield, 1981, p. 1).

To those who did not live through it but were born after it, or to those whose memories extended beyond it to the poverty and depression before the war, it was obvious in retrospect that the long boom was unique. It was the mistake of those who lived through it and were born into it to assume that living standards would continue to rise for ever and that mechanisms of economic control had been discovered that could avert any return to the periodic booms and slumps of the past. It is hard to recall now that, as Coates and Silburn (1970, p. 13) stated,

> During the fifties the myth that widespread material poverty had been finally and triumphantly overcome was so universally current, so widely accepted by politicians, social commentators and the general public alike, that for a decade and more, public controversy and political discussion were engrossed by the new (and fundamentally more encouraging) problems of what people are still pleased to call the 'Affluent Society'.

'Affluent workers' were supposedly responsible for Labour's third successive defeat in 1959, even though the research on car workers in Luton by Goldthorpe and Lockwood (1969) found that more of them voted Labour than other manual workers. Their support for Labour was, however, conditional or 'instrumental', and their collective adherence to trade unions was undermined by their 'private' lifestyles and 'individualistic' outlook. But although the working class was changing, no one yet suggested that it had actually disappeared or had bidden it farewell, as Gorz was to do in the early 1980s. However, economic change continued to corrode 'the very foundations of the working class as traditionally understood, that is the men and women who got their hands dirty at work, mainly in the mines, factories, or working with, or around, some kind of engines' (Hobsbawm, 1969, p. 285). Three long-term tendencies, continued Hobsbawm, contributed to this throughout the twentieth century: '(1) the relative decline of "industry" as compared with tertiary employments like distribution, transport and various services; (2) the relative decline of manual as compared with "white-collar" or "clean handed" labour within each industry; (3) the decline of the characteristic nineteenth century industries with their unusually high demand for old-fashioned manual work' (pp. 285-6).

With this loss of manufacturing industry, even the limited superstructure of social services that had been created during the long period of growth was no longer sustainable. For Britain's economic base was insufficiently modernized to withstand the loss of its previously secure and privileged position in world markets plunged into a new slump and assailed by numerous and more aggressive competitors. So the health service began to degenerate into a poor shadow of the private hospitals, public housing estates were reduced to new slums, and the state systems of insurance, benefits and pensions became new mechanisms for manipulating poverty and managing the poor.

Growing poverty aggravated by unemployment deepened insecurity for many while personal identities, the core of cultural *habitus* with its associated complex of acquired skills and values, were also shaken by the changing nature of the remaining employment. The futures in manual work, which many men in particular had anticipated, if not with pleasure then perhaps with a perverse pride, could no longer be guaranteed. These were the occupations in which, as Zuboff (1988) wrote, 'the body . . . [was] the source of both effort and skill', in which 'the pain and physical alteration that resulted from such exertion were inseparable from the subtle and complex skills from which a craftsperson derived pride and economic power' (pp. 37-8).

Worse, the few jobs that were now available in offices and shops had previously been considered only as part-time and 'women's work'. In what was left of manufacturing, technical change also had the effect of changing the type of labour required: as Massey (1983, p. 23) noted, 'The archetypal shift is from male manual workers classified as skilled to female assemblers classified as unskilled or semiskilled.' The largest apprenticeship remaining by the end of the 1980s, for instance, was in hairdressing. More girls began to stay on at school or go to further education college to train for office work while contemporaneously some professional occupations opened to women for the first time, so that more and more middle-class girls joined their brothers in higher education. By 1985, 43.5 per cent of all further and higher education students were female, rising towards the majority in the 1990s. Thus the expansion of the service sector resulted in a relative if not absolute improvement in women's overall labour market position. Although repeated studies showed the reluctance of unemployed men to take over women's dual role of houseworker when women also became in many households the sole breadwinners, the new economic situation plus the demands of an autonomous women's movement increasingly challenged the traditional stereotype of 'men's work'. This 'feminization of male labour' led to confused reactions from men, from an aggressive assertion of masculinity to accommodation with the changing reality by the so-called 'new man'.

Another dimension of the rapidly altering situation was provided by race. The second generation of black people increasingly rejected what many of them called the 'shit work' that had been accepted by their parents. Many British-born blacks and Asians also rejected the inner-city state schooling that led only to such dead-end jobs, but others - particularly many young black women and whole sections of the Asian communities - used the upsurge in educational credentials to compete for non-manual positions in the expanding service sector. Meanwhile, many white workers were squeezed out of the contracting skilled manual sector into aggravated competition for jobs they, or their parents, had previously abandoned as fit only for immigrant labour.

Again reactions were confused (for a contemporary record, see Clarke and Jefferson, 1975) but were not solely represented by the 'lads' learning to labour, whose racism and sexism were romanticized by Willis (1977) as somehow typical of all 'working class kids'. His study, widely accepted at the time and still influential, was a caricature, reminiscent of Emily Brontë's description in *Wuthering Heights* of Heathcliff, who 'when he found he must necessarily sink beneath his former level, then personal appearance sympathised with mental deterioration: he acquired a slouching gait and ignoble look; his naturally reserved disposition was exaggerated into an almost idiotic moroseness; and he took grim pleasure, apparently, in exciting the aversion rather than the esteem of his few acquaintance'.

Similarly, it was only a minority of working-class young women who found compensation for their unemployment in early child-rearing, as it had been predicted that the majority would by Griffin (whose 1985 study set out to replicate a female version of Willis's even more limited sample). Again Mrs Thatcher was to express more directly what such sociological studies alleged, that 'These single young girls deliberately become pregnant in order to jump a housing queue and get welfare payments' (*The Times*, 10 November 1988). Thus, supposed female working-class 'immorality' was the equivalent of the 'threat' to respectable society of male working-class violence. This was hardly borne out by national figures, as the average age of marriage continued to rise for all classes and the percentage of teenage pregnancies fell, although births out of wedlock have soared owing to the fact of cohabitation generally preceding if not (yet?) replacing formal marriage (see Ainley, 1991, p. 5).

Both Griffin and Willis, and other sociologists, therefore attributed to the entire working class attitudes and behaviour that were later alleged to typify only a section of it – the supposed 'underclass' at the very bottom of society. This might have been what many people wanted to believe was happening to the majority of the old working class but it served only to obscure further a rapidly changing reality. In this confused and confusing situation a new and not exclusively manual working class was being reformed in relation to, and partly merged with, the old non-manual middle class, which was also transformed by the changing fundamental division between manual and mental labour.

TOWARDS MASS MULTISKILLING?

As has been suggested, 'It is not easy to disentangle the influence of any one factor in determining changes in the occupational structure, as the effects of cyclical recession, longer range structural decline and technological displacement are often inextricably mixed' (Burgess, 1986). However, during the 1980s, as a result of a combination of these and other influences, it became apparent that fundamental changes had taken place in the work undertaken by many of the employed population. For technicians, for instance, 'In many fields knowledge over a broader range of disciplines is sought with more emphasis being placed on diagnostic competence', so that 'technologists increasingly find themselves fulfilling part-managerial functions and work in multi-disciplinary environments [where] a broader range of competence and systems awareness is also demanded' (Burgess, 1986). Their situation is thus similar to that of remaining craft workers who, it has been noted, are increasingly expected to acquire multiskills across a range of previously discrete activities, especially fault diagnosis and maintenance of more capital-intensive, automated and sophisticated machinery. The result is that, with the exception of some specialist sectors like aerospace, craft labour has been virtually reduced to maintenance and toolmaking, just as the decline in technicians' work relates closely to the virtual disappearance of traditional draughtsmen.

'New technology', as Burgess's colleague Brady similarly summarized,

> has resulted in the blurring of many traditional organisational boundaries [and if] defining 'skill' is difficult in relation to manufacturing occupations, it is even harder in relation to most service occupations . . . Many of the previously separate areas of clerical and administrative work are becoming integrated, with one person now undertaking a variety of tasks where several persons would have been employed in the past. New technology is resulting in the need for some jobs requiring a combination of selling, clerical and administrative skills.
>
> (Brady, 1984)

The *OECD Observer* of 10 November 1990, reviewing the effects of the diffusion of manufacturing technology in a variety of industrial sectors and across a number of developed countries, confirmed the general observation that 'there is a decline in the numbers of unskilled and semi-skilled workers in manufacturing and an increase in the numbers of professional engineers, technicians and similarly qualified staff required'. A second trend that it identified

> is towards increased convergence, with the shift from single skills towards the multiskills that are required to support increasingly integrated and interdependent technologies . . . The third move is towards improved flexibility of employment . . . The central element here is the ability – or agility – to switch to different skills as and where relevant . . . Such 'learning to learn' depends principally on developing a gradually deepening understanding of the broader context in which the worker is operating.

It is upon such summaries that optimistic scenarios regarding the effects of the application of information technology have been built. In them, as Zuboff (1988) showed, the skills of operatives are enhanced as they develop an overall view of the entire process of which previously they had only understood a part. Their new situation thus comes to overlap that of middle management, who, in some cases, seem to be left almost without a role. Hirschhorn (1986), another American, also had an optimistic expectation of the general levelling-up effect upon the workforce he anticipated from the introduction of new technology.

At an earlier stage of US use of new technology, Braverman (1974) had presented the contrasted pessimistic scenario (see p. 23). This was widely echoed in Britain, for example by Kumar (1978), who saw 'the dividing line between conception and execution of tasks, between hand and brain, continuing its relentless way up the technical hierarchy, deskilling the many and elevating the few' (p. 268). Pessimism is tempered, however, as has been observed, by a compromise position in which the effect of new technology is seen as enhancing the skills of a secure, regularly employed core while deskilling a mass of peripheral workers. In this version of events peripheral employment is often identified with the service sector. It is true that during the long post-war boom service sector employment grew more slowly than did manufacturing industry but, when manufacturing faltered, service employment sustained its rate of growth throughout the 1973–86 recession (though not into the succeeding recession from 1989 on). As a result, by 1984, 65 per cent of jobs were in servicing, employing just over half of all male workers and eight out of ten female, half of them working part-time. However, 'The effects of these shifts in employment are complex. The workforce in the service sector is highly diverse spanning as it does the spectrum from high level professions to unskilled manual or clerical jobs' (MSC, 1985, p. 72). In addition, the OECD (1981) drew attention to a significant general trend within this service sector growth, in pointing out that the majority worked in information occupations, defined as those occupations whose primary purpose is the production, processing or distribution of information or the infrastructure to support such tasks. Such figures supported the contention, for example of Brown and Senker (1982), that there had been 'a fundamental shift to a post-industrial information society'.

It might be supposed that across the service sector distinctions might be made between those working with people, in shops for instance, with pieces of paper, or at screens and keyboards in offices, as opposed to those using their hands to shift things about in transportation or stacking shelves in supermarkets. This would preserve the old manual/mental (dirty/clean) division that has in part broken down in manufacturing. However, as seen, many of the new service sector jobs combine working with things with working with people, especially as much of the work with things is actually taken on by the customer in self-service. In offices, the effects of the introduction of new technology have not so far been increased deskilling and unemployment, as was widely predicted. Partly this is because of the continued growth in office work – far many more people now work in offices (bureaus) in the advanced capitalist countries of the West than were ever employed in them in the old bureaucracies of the East. But within offices many workers have seen their roles enhanced in similar ways to other service workers and to the remaining manufacturing workers. The dreaded typing pool, for example, has virtually become a thing of the past and some secretaries, especially personal secretaries who always organized much of their bosses' work in the manner of an efficient alter ego, have seen partial recognition of their roles.

Although it is clear that a dual system of recruitment operates within the service sector, the old clean/dirty, mental/manual divide could hardly be re-erected upon the basis of employment conditions and career prospects. Many clerical and lower-level administrative office jobs are filled by workers who have limited career prospects and are typically female, often returning to work part-time after marriage. It is here that the fragmented and functionally specialized routine roles are concentrated when there is deskilling concomitant with re- and multiskilling in the use of new technology. On the other hand, for many of the married women involved, their jobs entail a trade-off in which the convenience of part-time work, however lowly paid and however poor their conditions, enables them to combine paid employment and (unpaid) domestic labour. Even if they and others do not regard their work as 'a proper job', the distinction between even these workers and their managers, or between the rank and file and the 'fast track' graduate recruits, who may for a time work alongside them, is not one between mental and manual work, since both are engaged in the same non-manual employment. This does not mean, of course, that people are unaware of the considerable status differences between them, just that these are now elaborated upon a different basis. This is often founded upon educational credentials, which also reflect class distinctions, but indirectly. The immediacy of the old, clear-cut mental/manual, clean/dirty, middle/working class division is thus obscured.

Moreover, the same flexibility demanded of manufacturing workers is asked of service workers, so that, as summarized by a bank training instructor quoted in Kirchner *et al.* (1984, p. 70), for example, 'Whereas in former times one part of our staff mainly carried out manual tasks – operating an adding machine, for example – and others performed cognitive tasks in administration and yet others needed social skills to work behind the counter as advisors and canvassers, our future employee will have to have all three skills to operate machines, deal with transactions and successfully advise customers.' Here too, as in manufacturing, the most significant impact of new technology may be upon the role of managers, especially middle managers. 'Management' is already not what it was, despite (or because of) the previous growth in middle management, particularly in small firms where, in industry, technologists and managers are becoming indistinguishable. Managerial authority is challenged by the wider dissemination through computers of information to which they could previously claim privileged access, or at least some specialist understanding derived from education and/or experience. Even senior executives, who have been able to preserve 'the orality of their culture' (Zuboff, 1988, p. 178) through business lunches, golf clubs, etc., are threatened by a technology that can render the opacity of these informal business dealings down into itemized and transparent symbols for all to see.

How far the old hand and brain, skilled and unskilled divisions have disintegrated in a core in which management and workers share manual and mental tasks, as well as canteens and the same white overalls (as on the Japanese model), is debatable. It implies that employment can be guaranteed for a core of secure workers, a doubtful supposition in times of seemingly endemic financial crises for an increasingly marginal and insecure national economy. It also indicates their segregation from a new periphery of temporarily employed, flexible workers. This periphery is seen as more or less large – from 70 per cent, and thus including all or most of the old working class, down to a 10 or 20 per cent 'underclass' of more or less permanent unemployables. If such 'skill polarization' is taking place, it is 'linked to the increasing fragmentation of low-level work . . . which is also associated with the growth of part-time employment' (Burgess, 1986). So 'The use of new technology has been accompanied by a shift towards non-career and part-time recruitment at the lower level of jobs, particularly in the financial sector and in retailing and distribution' (Brady, 1984). Hakim (1987) estimated the size of what she called 'the flexible workforce' at one-third of total employment in 1987. This included not only part-time workers (the largest element, estimated at 6.5 million in 1991, and constituted mostly of older women) but also temporary contract workers, those working flexible hours, job sharers, the early retired, home workers and the self-employed, with considerable overlap between the groups. The notion of being an employee for whom an employer has, or ought to have, some sort of responsibility is lost to all these independent, subcontracted, self-employed who have to be responsible for themselves.

'In terms of numbers the flexible workforce is concentrated in the service sector industries such as hotels and catering, distribution, repairs and professional and business services' (Hakim, 1987), amounting to 68 per cent of employment in catering, cleaning, hairdressing and other personal service occupations. 'Selling work is also dominated by flexible rather than traditional work patterns.' Despite the growth of this 'flexible sector' during the 1980s, Hakim noted that it was not a new phenomenon but the result of 'very long-term trends [that] have been leading to a major restructuring of the labour force which is only now becoming visible by the sheer magnitudes involved'. Flexible working was not therefore purely a response to recession that would disappear if ever there were a permanent recovery. Indeed, some of the prophets of post-modern, post-industrial, post-Fordist information society have seen flexible work as the type of all future employment. It is linked by them particularly to the decline of organized labour – trade union membership in the UK dropped from 13 to 10 million during the 1980s as flexible working also increased rapidly. However, the effects of flexible work contracts are seen as more far-reaching, so that they permeate every aspect of the new society. For example, Lyotard (1979, p. 66) suggested that 'The temporary contract is in practice supplanting permanent institutions in the professional, emotional, sexual, cultural, family, and international domains, as well as in political affairs.'

Whether such claims are valid in reality depends first upon how far the new flexible worklife that supposedly gives rise to them has in fact supplanted traditional employment. Various writers have accused the post-Fordists of over-generalizing on the very limited basis of just a few industrial regions, typically Emilia-Romagna in Italy. John Lovering (1989), for example, reviewing economic restructuring in Britain in the 1980s, concluded that so far there was only 'a perfunctory sort of Post-Fordism'. Like others, he indicated that where flexible methods had been introduced, both in manufacture and in employment contracts, they coexisted with traditional mass production lines and their associated collective wage bargaining, even though management had successfully imposed individual contracts in other areas where formerly unions had been strong, for example in printing and journalism. Although favoured by the Conservative governments' preference for local – plant-by-plant and individual – work contracts, including performance-related pay and privatized health and pension schemes, a completely flexible economy is neither inevitable nor perhaps possible. Technology can be utilized either to encourage it, or to move in an opposite direction towards more democratic accountability and collective control based upon wider access to previously privileged information.

Of course, segmented or dual labour markets have always existed. As Harvey (1989, p. 152) pointed out:

> While it is true that the declining significance of union power has reduced the singular power of white male workers in monopoly sector markets, it does not follow that those excluded from those labour markets, such as blacks, women, ethnic minorities of all kinds, have achieved sudden parity (except in the sense that many traditionally privileged white male workers have been marginalised alongside them). While some women and some minorities have gained access to more privileged positions, the new labour market conditions have for the most part re-emphasised the vulnerability of disadvantaged groups.

'So what else is new?', Alex Callinicos asked in his 'Marxist critique' *Against Postmodernism* (1989). He and the traditional left continue to assert that nothing fundamental has changed. For them, the tripartite class world is still in place; there is no essential division within the working class, nor between it and a more or less ideologically constructed underclass. Only a 'new middle class' has augmented the old middle class between the boss employers and their workers. Yet the appeals of the traditional left to the working class they claim to represent sound increasingly hollow to the working people to whom they are addressed. The new model Labour Party abandoned the last of its proletarian pretensions in elusive search of the electoral middle ground it lost in the 1992 general election, while the various 'Militant' and 'Real Labour' candidates did only marginally better and were decisively rejected at the 1991 Walton by-election on Merseyside.

Between the old left position that nothing has changed and the new left, 'new times' argument that everything has changed to a new post-Fordist, post-industrial, post-capitalist, information society, it is surely correct to assert that some things have changed but not that everything has changed. Especially with the decline of Keynesian 'demand' management of economies that are now less 'mixed' in the way they once were, it is obvious that we still live in a free-market, capitalist society. Indeed, 'free' economies celebrate themselves as such in contrast to the failure of command economic planning in countries that claimed to be socialist. In such free-market societies, as Offe (1985, p. 2) wrote, 'the labour market, which treats labour power as a commodity, constitutes the most significant feature'.

The long-term trends that have been noted have changed the nature of much employment available in the labour market. The relative decline of manufacturing has undermined the traditional divisions of industrial labour associated with it (non-manual, skilled and unskilled manual). Flexible working with new technology has blurred the boundaries of the great divide between manual and mental labour in both the secondary (manufacturing) and tertiary (service) sectors. The continued rise of service and flexible working has brought more women into employment, if only part-time, and has 'feminized' much remaining employment for men. The expansion of office and white-collar work has brought new opportunities for clean, non-manual work in growing and new professions not only to the children of the old middle class but also to people whose parents were, and perhaps still consider themselves and are considered by their children as, traditionally working class. Traditional working-class communities are, however, no longer sustained by the old industrial concerns that brought them together in ship-building, docking, steel-working, mining and along the production lines of gargantuan factories and Babylonian mills. Their break-up and dispersal has been under way since the large-scale redevelopment of the 1960s, which has done much to alter traditional cultural forms of local working-class life. These have become more regulated by national norms communicated by the mass media. Traditional working-class communities survive now only around the remaining mines or other primary areas, such as the villages of the East Neuk of Fife, though the work in fishing here also tends towards multiskilling with new technology and self-employment, while homes are generally owned and no longer tied.

Home ownership has to a degree broken up even some of the huge working-class city estates and districts, though these were always riven with conflicts between religions and nationalities, as well as between 'good' areas and 'bad', the respectable and the rough. Private home ownership does not in any case necessarily directly affect class consciousness or political allegiance, and often does no more than transfer rent payments to a public or private landlord into mortgage repayments to a building society. The nature of the relationship becomes brutally clear with growing mortgage default and subsequent mass repossessions.

Productive labour still occupies very many people and its technology has not become so sophisticated that flexible manufacture is the norm, nor is it likely to become so in production for a mass market. Even where flexible production has been introduced, making individually ordered and customized cars for instance, it does not necessarily do away with production lines, as confirmed by a visit to the Ford plant at Dagenham, which is still the largest in Europe but small compared to its parent in Detroit. Alongside such robotics and other state-of-the-art machinery, the recrudescence of quite primitive and grossly exploitative employment in sweatshops under paternal management, of child labour and new types of domestic service, is a marked feature of the metropolitan economies. If the majority of people are no longer employed in making things, however, but in office and service work, this does not mean that the working lives and conditions of all or even most of us have been enhanced in recent years. For most of us, even though it still provides some sense of participation in the larger social world, work continues to be an alienating experience we undertake only in order to pursue our own personal aims and ambitions. These continue to be defined for the majority in terms of our private or family life and not in terms of our public lives or careers. While there has certainly been a decline in working-class political cultures, and mass marketing has encouraged an increasingly privatized lifestyle, this alienation too is not new. Even in times of full employment, there were a large number of unskilled and semi-skilled 'dead-end jobs', as they were called, while the quality of Fordist production on the line was notoriously mind-numbing.

What has made many people's employment situation worse is the chronic insecurity affecting nearly all levels of the labour hierarchy. This is prompted not only by increasingly rapid technical and organizational change but also by the persistence of permanent, structural unemployment. Unlike the celebrated core (or corps) of company workers in Japan, very few people employed in Britain today are immune to the threat of relegation to the ranks of the unemployed, even if this is disguised by redundancy payments and early retirement. In this sense the core–periphery model is also decidedly limited. However, it may be that a new and different periphery exists, not only geographically in the depressed regions and in districts within even economically buoyant areas but also socially in relation to a more or less politically and ideologically sustained 'underclass'.

In order to consider this possibility, and the effects of the changes that there have been in the class structure, the concern with skill outlined in Chapter 2, especially its cultural dimensions, can be brought together with the outline history of class in this chapter. Here changes in the skills exercised at work have been shown to be influential upon class divisions, particularly the old distinction between manual and mental work that has now been considerably erased. The new class culture can best be approached by way of the recurrent discussion of 'skill shortages'. These have repeatedly been held responsible for the failure of attempts to modernize the economy. They are related to the 'cultural blockage' that has also been considered such a brake upon the modernization of the British economy and society.

Chapter 4

'Skill Shortages' and Class Cultures

It is depressing that mass unemployment and skill shortages exist side by side.
(Report of the Employment Committee of the House of Commons, 1984)

WHOSE 'SKILLS SHORTAGE'?

In 1990 Mark Corney and I wrote *Training for the Future: The Rise and Fall of the Manpower Services Commission*. Apart from John Fairley's account of the MSC in Scotland (1990) and Brendan Evans's *Politics of the Training Market* (1992), which takes the story forward to the founding of the Training and Enterprise Councils, this is still the only historical account of this remarkable institution. Yet the MSC at one time employed nearly 30,000 people spending £3 billion a year to administer a plethora of training and employment schemes directly or indirectly, involving more than a million workers, most of whom would otherwise have been unemployed. The MSC was specifically created to link job creation with training for employment in a state-directed manpower planning effort that was unprecedented in peacetime. This amounted, as Professor Ken Roberts wrote in his introduction to the book, 'to *the* major attempt at large-scale social engineering in Britain since the wave of post-war measures'. More remarkable still, this quasi-autonomous and partly non-governmental organization thrived under the Thatcher regime's opposition to corporatism and commitment to a labour market free from state interference. Yet in 1988, just after the quango had been poised to take over all of education and training and unite them in a new super-ministry, the MSC was abolished as the government reversed the cross-party commitment to a vocational education policy that there had been since 1976. It was then seriously proposed by Mrs Thatcher to her last party conference that the battle for the economic future could be won, not by relating education to employment and training, but 'in Britain's classrooms' by teaching the future generations of workers to spell properly! Little changed in her party's education policy after she left. State-subsidized training was returned to employers, whose failure to train had previously led to the creation of the Industrial Training Boards, which preceded the MSC and the last of which was abolished in 1991.

At the end of the narration of these extraordinary events, we commented that 'After nearly fifteen years (from 1973 to 1988) and an estimated £25 billion expenditure (at a conservative estimate) there was still a "skills crisis" in the British economy. Indeed, skill training in British industry all but ceased. The result was that as soon as the economy picked up temporarily, as it did after passing through the trough of 1986, skill shortages became manifest and were said to be strangling industrial development' (Ainley and Corney, 1990, p. 93). Thus, despite the obsession with identifying skill shortages and attempting to eradicate them, 'skills mismatch' was again held to account for the bottleneck that held back industrial advance and the full use of new technology. This, in turn, contributed to the weakness of the recovery and its vulnerability to the next world slump. As the next recession deepened, the *OECD Economic Outlook* once more reported 'chronic skill shortages and inadequate training of the labour force' in Britain (July 1991). The report echoed an early world competitiveness survey, which ranked the UK bottom among OECD countries for standards of compulsory education, availability of skilled labour and qualified engineers. The country was also ranked last for in-company training (reported in Working Brief, August/September 1991). Contrary to previous claims that a 'training revolution' had taken place in employer attitudes, which justified the establishment of the TECs, training was once again the first casualty of recession as redundancies suddenly succeeded skill shortages. It is predictable that, with another turn of the screw, skill shortages and 'overheating' will set in at an even earlier stage than after the last recession.

> 'In sunny Loseland (London and the South East) this phenomenon took on grotesque dimensions [in the partial and accidental recovery upon which the economy stumbled in the mid-1980s], as firms paid unusually high salaries to attract skilled staff. One insurance company even paid its employees a handsome premium if they could recruit their friends and relatives for office work. These shortages coexisted [in the capital] with the largest concentration of unemployed people in Europe and second in the world only to São Paulo and Mexico City. Instead of asking why, after all the money that had been spent by the MSC, the mass of London's unemployed had not been trained to occupy these vacant posts, or why they spurned low-paid work in the hotel and catering trade where vacancies existed, the government as usual merely blamed the unemployed themselves for their laziness. The mismatches were used as an excuse to introduce benefit cuts for claimants who refused 'reasonable offers' of employment, thus preparing the way for national compulsory work for benefit programmes. [Yet] 'skill mismatch' was not only a consequence of inadequate training programmes but was also another symptom of the hardening of the economic arteries of Thatcher's Britain. Not only did the overheating of some local economies, combined with the stagnation of others, explain the weird discontinuities of economic development, but the interaction of the jobs and housing markets trapped both middle-income earners and the poor in depressed regions of the country and in deprived districts within even the most prosperous areas . . . [so that] government measures merely acted upon and exacerbated the already existing cleavages and interactions between discrete labour markets separated by age, gender, race and skill.
> (Ainley and Corney, 1990, pp. 94–5)

The government seems really to have believed its own rhetoric in the 1987 election that its policies had at last created an economic miracle. How else can one explain the cuts in training that followed, even while the then Chancellor John Major faithfully followed orders to drive the economy deliberately into deepening recession and unemployment rose again towards three million? Demographics encouraged the delusion that youth unemployment was after all cyclical and not structural, as the baby-boom generation of the early 1960s, whose members had found its way on to the labour market in the early 1980s, gave way to a new crisis fall in the numbers of young people. Youth training was thus abandoned as a coherent national scheme, and the new Training and Enterprise

Councils could, like the US Private Industry Councils on which they were modelled, concentrate on training for their participating employers' immediate needs without attempting to reskill and update the training of the entire workforce. A training market privately administered with public money in which the government has divested itself of any responsibility for developing adequate skills for the workforce had thus been created, presaging extension of the same principle to the whole of education.

Focusing on training the employed at the expense of the unemployed was justified by a version of the 'trickle down' theory with which Conservative governments argued that stimulating the private sector and rewarding already wealthy entrepreneurs would have the eventual effect of contagiously benefiting everyone around them. In this case it was hoped that a 'skills ladder' could be created by in-house training in private industry, which would lead to promotion for those involved, so creating more wealth and, ultimately, vacancies at the lowest levels that the unemployed would then fill, climbing the ladder in their turn. The strategy ignored the persistence of 'jobless growth', by which the use of new technology, even if it involves more training and investment in its use, does not necessarily mean more people are employed to work it; indeed the opposite is more likely to be the case as capital expenditure can be justified by savings in labour costs. For skills to 'trickle down the ladder', there is explicit reliance only on larger companies; there is no reason for the small and medium-size companies, with fewer than twenty and fewer than 200 employees respectively, which together provide the majority of employment, to change their traditional short-term attitudes to training, and they will go on poaching skilled staff as required and when they can afford it. Conflicts between the Department of Employment and the TECs it set up have resulted in the trading off of inadequate budgets for a flexibility that enabled TECs to disregard their responsibility for the needs of the unemployed, disabled and disadvantaged in their areas. Yet with the return of recession, such were the numbers of the marginalized and 'peripheral' people in the inner cities and the regions that they could not be ignored, especially when they emphasized their presence by aggressively rioting.

'Skill shortages', no less than 'skills', mean many things to many people and the language of 'skills shortages' fails to address the needs of the unemployed, because it is expressed in terms of employers' demands. These are not necessarily the same thing, despite the fact that employers want skilled workers and the unemployed want work, ideally with training and good prospects. As the journal of the further education lecturers' union, whose members now undertake most of the skills training for industry and commerce that has survived since the demise of apprenticeships, said, 'The evidence of skills shortages understates and oversimplifies the consequences of the failure of our education and training' (December 1990). For at the same time that there are three million unemployed, half of them young and a third of them long-term unemployed, there are specific skills shortages for professional grades in electronics engineering, for test technicians, systems analysts, technical authors, design, development and sales engineers. There is also under-recruitment for chemical, electronic and mechanical engineering courses at higher education level, where graduate unemployment coexists with employers' complaints that they cannot get the graduates they want to fill specific vacancies.

This last fact provides a handle to begin to get hold of this slippery problem, for students cannot be forced to study science and engineering if they prefer arts and humanities. Women can also be encouraged to enter engineering as a career, but the factors that cause them to drop out from it at every level, from their choice of GCSEs onward, can hardly be addressed without profound social and cultural change. Similarly illustrative is what Peter Robinson called the 'Docklands paradox':

> Create some 10,000 jobs in the London Docklands or an equivalent location and only a fraction appear to go to local residents, as opposed to people newly arriving or commuting in. One explanation is that local residents might not have the skills to fill the jobs being created. However, an equally important explanation for the 'Docklands paradox' would focus on the way employers recruit and the discrimination, both direct and indirect, which permeates employers' recruitment practices.
> (Robinson, 1992, p. 7)

Many long-term unemployed people have good relevant skills. These skills are embodied in cultural forms that allow their transmission between generations. These skills of productive life are not limited to the workplace or to paid labour, but at the workplace it is workers who train workers, not employers or 'industry'. It is only in dialogue with this existing practical knowledge that any technical progress takes place at all, let alone artistic and scientific development. However, without work, training is left in a social vacuum and skills transfer through culture atrophies and dies. When education attempts to fill this vacuum the bad experiences that many unemployed people have had with their previous academic schooling mean that many will not even consider a formal training option. They want jobs and may be desperate enough to take a job at any price but, like most people, what they would really like are jobs with prospects of progression and development that use their talents and abilities to the full.

For many unemployed people, their experience has also taught them that 'training' is too often a euphemism for unemployment relief. As Swann and Turnbull observed as early as 1978, 'In the past the able bodied poor were set to work [but] in recent years this phrase has been replaced by the euphemism of training' (p. 162). With the exception of a few select Youth Training Schemes, like those that were run by Information Technology Centres, and the long-defunct Training Opportunities Programme, which offered speculative training to the unemployed in response to individual wishes, the organization of training for the unemployed has stigmatized those enrolled in it. State programmes sustain the belief of even the founder of social insurance, William Beveridge, in 'good and wholesome discipline for the un- and under-employed' (Beveridge, 1909, p. 233). They have their origin in the Victorian workhouse, resurrected in the regional aid programmes of the inter-war years when correctional training centres were established to keep the unemployed off the streets, lest the devil found work for idle hands. As youth unemployment in particular rose in the 1970s, the same concern was expressed in sociological enquiry into whether unemployed people might lose their 'work ethic'. Notwithstanding repeated evidence finding that, despite the deleterious physical and psychological effects of prolonged unemployment, this fear was unfounded, government effort persisted in averting the possibility by a succession of make-work schemes. Unfortunately, employers share this belief in the inherent 'laziness' of the unemployed. They think that the longer people are unemployed the more they lose valued attitudes of punctuality and compliance. As a result a vicious circle is set up so that the longer someone is unemployed the harder it is for him or her to get work. These attitudes are supported by the almost constant drizzle of stories in the tabloid and local press about 'social security scroungers', stimulated by periodic and well-publicized DSS investigation of what is invariably very minor fraud.

Above all, employers do not see themselves as responsible for either educating or retraining the unemployed, which they regard as a social problem not of their concern. As the *Financial Times* put it, 'successful businessmen are not educators. Businessmen are necessarily driven by short-termism' (editorial, 5 December 1990). Firms aim to maximize profit as their primary aim and they often calculate that short-term profit is more likely to flow from poaching trained workers from elsewhere than from spending money on training them themselves:

> In the great majority of companies training is not a Board level matter. Most of the chief executives have a limited interest in what training is taking place in their company . . . Expenditure on training is very rarely seen or treated as an investment in any financial sense . . . Training expenditure is not seen as an investment expected to lead to an identifiable income stream, but more as an overhead which can, like building maintenance, be reduced when times are hard.
> (Coopers & Lybrand survey for the MSC, 1991, p. 248)

Most firms do not therefore undertake countercyclical expenditure to produce training for stock during downturns so as to avoid skills bottlenecks with any economic upturn. Nor do most of them have strategies for in-firm training that reach throughout the entire organization (see Corney, 1991). Some employers have even shown a reluctance to train their employees to the levels recommended by government through the National Council for Vocational Qualifications on the grounds that such recognition of employees' competencies would only fuel their wage demands.

Britain's employers should not be singled out for blame in this regard, however. Although their reluctance to train has been repeatedly noted, this is not because they are more 'greedy' and 'short-sighted' than their German and Japanese competitors, with whom they are so often unfavourably compared and who have always been firmly committed to vocational education and training, even when their economies were weak. Rather, general explanations for Britain's comparative backwardness in education and training derive from the legacy of industrial primacy. The initial lack of competitors and, later, the protection of empire meant that Britain enjoyed early economic success without the state intervention, particularly in the organization of education and training, that was required for other countries to catch up. As the situation eventually became critical a severely reduced manufacturing base was increasingly exposed to foreign competition. Skills shortages were then blamed on rates of pay for apprentices, which were, as the Conservative-controlled House of Commons Employment Committee complained in 1979, 'so near to those for craftsmen as to deter employers from offering apprenticeships'. Next year the MSC's *Outlook on Training* argued that the root of Britain's training problem was poor utilization of labour: 'Many of the assumed skills shortages were not in fact the result of training inadequacies, but rather of the under-utilisation of skilled labour with many trained workers employed in jobs requiring little skill, the maintenance of craft status for work which no longer merited it and the poor mobility of labour' (MSC, 1980, para. 3.3-6).

This last diagnosis was nearer to the mark, and it was part of the vision of the MSC, or at least some of its leading officers, that the historic opportunity provided by the rapid development of new technology should be made full use of to create a new system of education and training. For the first time this would relate formal, academic study to practical, applied learning in a unified vocational system. Unlike the latest education reforms, stemming from the 1988 Act, this would aim at demolishing the traditional divisions between selection for an elite education for the professions and practical training for the crafts. Such a new, unified system of modernized schooling and apprenticeship would undermine and eventually abolish the class barriers that are sustained by an outdated division of labour at work. At the same time new and more equal social relations could only promote the modernization and revitalization of the economy, leading to a new industrial revolution. This in turn would stimulate the most effective use of new technology, which not only has the potential to lighten and diversify labour by automating tedious and arduous tasks, but also has an information producing and disseminating capacity. As Hirschhorn and Zuboff have shown, this requires a sharing of resources and information among operatives and an extension of their creative abilities in new relationships. The development of technology thus has the potential not only to simplify tasks but also to allow them to be shared and integrated, increasing productivity with less laborious and repetitive effort. It thus presents a real opportunity for the transformation of the ancient division between workers by hand and by brain.

The MSC's desire to create a new attitude towards training implied a need to look beyond the myopic definition of the problem in terms of skill shortages and to break the old connection between training and unemployment. Unfortunately, because the MSC as a state agency typically posed its perception of the problem in class-neutral and purely technical terms, it became drawn into doing precisely the opposite of what it intended, so that throughout the 1980s it was used by government to manipulate and occupy the unemployed. It also became involved with the Conservative government's persistent feud with the trade unions, so that the MSC's advocacy of 'flexibility' and 'modernized apprenticeships for all' became part of the government's 'deregulation' strategy for 'freeing markets and increasing competition'. Although the rhetoric might be different, it cannot be confidently predicted that a Labour government's resurrection of the quango in the form of a Ministry for Education and Training would have any other effect; especially as the heightened selective effects of the increasingly academic and vocationally irrelevant 1988 education reforms are unlikely to be checked.

It now becomes clear that 'the skills problem', expressed primarily as 'skills shortages' for narrow employer demands and not as the need of the majority to use and develop their skills to the full for the benefit of society, is in fact a class problem. More specifically, it is one of sustaining outdated class divisions, based primarily upon the eroded distinction between manual and mental labour. This is nowhere clearer than in the case of employers' demands, which, when they are not for specific key workers, are couched at a level of vagueness and generality that make them very hard to grasp. 'Initiative', 'responsibility', 'the ability to learn to learn' and such nebulous terms mean different things at different levels of employment. At the lowest level they can mean putting up with mind-numbing boredom, low wages, disgusting conditions and degrading treatment. As far as customer relations are concerned, they too often imply American-style superficialities aiming to please the customer, who is always right. Expressed in the US business school language of 'functional role analysis' as the criterion for vocational qualification, they too often let slip the bottom line of their 'mission statements', which is always to maximize profits. Even here though, especially at the level at which organizational change begins to impinge upon traditional divisions of status and authority within companies, employers are unwilling to substantiate the rhetoric of their employment demands. It has been seen how the most effective use of new technology blurs the fundamental division between manual and mental work, shop-floor and office, operator and manager. Yet the personal investment in managerial authority is just too great even to begin doing this. It is not only material interests in career positions in the hierarchy that are at stake, but also ideological conviction in the whole purpose of working to produce a profit regardless of other social considerations. This would be thrown into question by a genuine participation of the majority of the workforce in the management of the enterprise. Thus, despite the rhetoric, conventional divisions are sustained, reflex reactions are reinforced and traditional authority is preserved. What it would mean for the opposite to be the case can be seen by looking broadly at the situation from the point of view of a real information society.

INFORMATION SOCIETY

There is a lot of loose talk about the information society of the future. The notion is connected to the overextended idea that history is moving beyond industrialism, or at least beyond industry organized along the lines of mass production, as it has been since Ford set up his Model T assembly line in 1913. Instead of directly consuming the products of nature as in primary (agricultural) production, or acting upon materials to transform them into finished products as in secondary (industrial) production, society is supposedly moving into a third phase in which new technology enables individuals to work upon a new raw material in the form of data to change disordered symbols of reality into ordered information. In this third phase of social evolution, with its accompanying third wave of technological development – for some reason these things are always presented as coming in threes – information is seen as the main source of wealth and power. Somehow it is supposed that whole societies can exist by their members exchanging information with one another. In the more fantastic versions of this future the lucky information workers, who all seem to be self-employed, somehow gain the means of life by swapping information with each other telematically through a network architecture of integrated systems. They carry their workstations with them and work wherever they are – in the car, on the beach or at home – transmitting and receiving signals through terminals as small as a wrist-watch. Such was, for example, Shirley Williams's vision of 'the impact of tomorrow's technology on work and society' in her *A Job to Live* (1985).

Information theory, to which such speculations are only loosely related, may have been stimulated by the mathematical modelling facilitated by modern computers but is not restricted to what Bateson (1978) called 'the noosphere', the growing body of cultural knowledge representing humanity's acquired experience in symbolic form. Rather, information or systems theory views all thermodynamic systems as involving exchanges of information. From this perspective, 'The way-of-life of a person is an entity with properties which are not reducible to the simple aggregate properties of its parts. On the contrary . . . the ways of life of people in the social classes acquire characteristics from being parts of a larger system which may be called the way-of-life of people in the whole society. Within the ways-of-life of the social classes distinct subsystems of the ways-of-life of e.g. occupational groups may be discerned' (Hassan, 1988, pp. 7–8). In this context human needs are defined in terms of sustaining the necessary conditions for the proper functioning of the system, and if they are not met the behaviour of the system is disturbed, either at the level of individual or group subsystem or at the level of the system as a whole. Energy and information are here synonymous.

Human beings are unique in not only being informed by but in forming their own environment through the use of tools. Tools transform objects not only literally but also conceptually; they distance consciousness from its immediate perceptions by forming a new purposive whole of means to end, with thought before action. A new and symbolic subsystem is thus created that is capable of self-steering. Unlike inherited genetic information and animal communication by signalling, symbolic consciousness and the self-steering system it creates are capable of learning from past mistakes to act differently in future. Therefore, 'It is a notable property of self-steering that the same state never returns in a self-steering system', as Aulin (1982, p. 84), who formulated these 'cybernetic laws of social progress', put it.

Aulin presumed that the ways-of-life of which individuals as self-steering systems are a part are themselves self-steering, and have not become what information theory describes as closed systems, which perpetually return to the state from which they started. Laborit, a biologist who used the same systems approach to humans as to other living beings, was not as sure that this could be taken for granted. He saw that hierarchies in society often operate solely to preserve their own power by closing systems in order to prevent any further development and to lock them into repeated identical cycles or loops. As he explained, 'Every closed information-structure at a given level of organisation can have only one finality, namely the preservation of this information structure' (Laborit, 1977, p. 129). Looking at the economic system of commodity production as such a system closed at the level of its own finality, Laborit asked, 'Is man programmed by evolution to be essentially a commodity producer?' (p. 125). For as he pointed out, 'Economic expansion is not, one imagines, a phenomenon that can go on forever within a biosphere that is limited in time and space, even if the day of reckoning is deferred by the discovery of new sources of energy or by the control of pollution and population' (p. 139). It is necessary therefore to break out of this particular closed system; otherwise, 'If we extrapolate from future trends, the human species has set course for destroying the biosphere itself' (p. 134). That this was not a paranoiac speculation is substantiated by even the Organisation for Economic Co-operation and Development, which recognized that 'the scale of man's activities and the pace of their development have now reached the point where the cumulative effects on the environment are undermining the delicate natural and geophysical equilibria of the entire planet' (Dorin, 1989).

Break-out can be achieved by opening the self-contained and closed subsystem of commodity production for the sake of producing more commodities in order to maximize profits to produce more profits . . . (and so on). If auto-destruction is to be avoided, the closed loop of production for profit must be opened to the larger ecological system within which it is contained and which it threatens to disrupt. Such integration will have 'to determine precisely how the mass and energy taken from the environment will have to circulate' in what Laborit called the planetary society, 'in order to ensure the maintenance of its global organisation, while at the same time ensuring the maintenance of all the individual elements which constitute it' (Laborit, 1977, p. 131).

This is not a call for the accumulation by a scientific technocracy of supposedly objective information in some vast database like that planned for the human genome project upon which scientists around the world are working. It is a call for the availability of the information necessary for individual members of society to become informed of their own function and purpose at the global level. This information goes beyond that necessary for individuals to be aware of their contribution to the production and sale of commodities or services for the sake of (from their point of view) maintaining and reproducing their own individual and family subsystems. The latter are in any case increasingly disrupted by the dysfunctions of the larger economic, social and ecological systems of which they are a part. The opening of specialized information systems that is necessary to integrate them with the widest possible system within which they are contained goes beyond closure at the level of individual enterprises in competition with each other. Otherwise, individuals' contributions are measured only in relation to the success or failure of their firms, regardless of any other consequences of their actions. Similarly, closure at the level of national economies, or the trading blocs and military alliances of which they are parts, must be opened to the global economy and the ecosphere that sustains it. Thus what Laborit meant by information society 'is not the specialised information which enables the individual to transform inanimate matter, nor the information supplied by manual or conceptual training, but a far more vast scale of information which concerns the importance of the individual as an individual within the human collectivity' (p. 68).

This is a considerably wider definition of information society than usual! It is, however, connected to conventional definitions by reliance upon the information technology that makes it possible. It is also related to the issue of democracy as self-steering. At present, the triumphalist West has elevated one form of limited representative democracy over every other virtue, save the 'freedom' and 'equality' with which it is coupled. It is doubtful, however, that the majority rules in any self-styled democracy beyond deciding between two not very different ways to accommodate itself to an economic system perpetually balanced on the verge of crisis. This metropolitan economy of production for the sake of producing more commodities can sustain its precarious position only by further competition to impoverish the people and degrade the environment of the majority of the world's population. Yet even the former socialist countries have abandoned their attempts to control the market economy in goods produced for sale and their leaders clamour to subordinate their social development to the dictates of international capitalism. Their societies can now be regarded as experiments that failed to organize alternative forms of democratic control over the anarchy of market production through planning that became increasingly bureaucratic and of benefit only to a new ruling class. Dogmatic and grandiose plans also dedicated to maximizing production rode roughshod over the wishes and aspirations of people and wreaked havoc upon the environment. Lenin thought it possible for the majority under socialism to control state capitalism, by using the techniques made available by modern banking and through communication by electric telegraph. Perhaps it was, though things did not turn out that way in the circumstances. Now that communications and computing provide new potential for planning and democratic control, perhaps a new historical opportunity presents itself. The goal, however, is no longer 'socialism' but simply survival. As the alternative is posed between survival and destruction, utopia has become reality.

Utopian ideals of a fixed end-state of human development, whether as communism, a free society or any other state of grace, can be forsaken. Instead, as Laborit suggested, we need to develop and implement the collective knowledge of what is required for human survival. New technology affords opportunities to do this by creating an information society in which meaning is given to the actions of individual members of society in relation to their most general finality at the level of planetary survival. New technology also has the potential to inform all citizens as generally as is possible, so that they can exercise democratic control in moving towards that agreed common goal. It is now widely accepted that the creation of supranational economic units, like the European Community, does not necessarily entail subordination to a bureaucratic centre but can allow regional and local autonomy within the larger whole. A Europe of regions is indeed anticipated. Again, new technology facilitates the interdependent relationships that will have to be developed between the whole and its parts.

Telecommunications and computing could then be used not only to reduce bureaucracy considerably, but also to increase participation and democracy. As Ian McLean (1989) wrote in his study of democracy and new technology, 'This technology unlocks many doors, some of them opening on to new democratic vistas' (p. 63). It brings 'broader and more satisfying forms of democracy into our grasp than ever before' (p. 171). As he described it, much of the machinery is already available to turn many of these possibilities into realities. For instance, 'The technology enabling the next British General Election to be entirely conducted by telephone is expected to be in place by 1992' (p. 150). This would put a phone in the home of every citizen, which in itself would go a long way to 'wire up' the entire society, especially if linked to microcomputers like the French Minitel. It would also greatly help the participation of disabled and elderly electors. Interactive televisions could also be used in the same manner, as well as to access and display information in the way that Prestel already does. For computer networks not only facilitate the recording and calculating of votes: potentially they also enable people to be better informed about the issues they are voting on. Further, by enhancing direct communication they could allow electors to make sure their representatives really represent them and facilitate their recall if they do not. As well as communication between electors and elected, teleconferencing can allow direct democracy to go beyond unwieldy and manipulable mass meetings. There are many possibilities, and local experiments should be started now to discover them and their limitations in the self-governance of as many areas of life as possible, let alone to reform an archaic national voting system popularly perceived as unfair. In another guise, as McLean pointed out, by lightening domestic and other labour new technology can give people more time in which to participate in democratic decisions; leisure time derived from slavery is a neglected aspect of democracy but was essential to its development, whether in ancient Greece or the revolutionary USA.

With regard to industrial democracy among those who work, but usually exert little control over the use of their labour power, it has been seen how computer-integrated manufacture (CIM), which is the logical extension of the computerization presently being applied piecemeal to production, offers new opportunities to integrate the work of all employees in an enterprise. While it requires fewer operatives (or the same numbers for less time), by storing information centrally CIM ensures that it is communicated to all. The more inputs there are to the system, from designers, engineers and managers, through repair and maintenance workers, plus those involved in storage and delivery, to sales and marketing staff, the more information is generated and the more effectively it may be integrated for decision-making that may also be computer-aided. As Hirschhorn (1986, p. 2) wrote: 'The computer answers queries put to it by the operating personnel regarding the short-run effects of variables at various control levels, but decisions are made by the operators. Operating personnel are provided with technical calculations and economic data, conventionally only available to technical staff, that support learning and self-regulation. In this manner operator learning is enhanced.' The logical form of organization for optimum performance becomes cooperative and non-hierarchical. Information is no longer specialized but generalized, for one part of the manufacturing process cannot act without informing and influencing all the others. The more that divisions between those who know and those who do, the executive and the rest, are effaced by everyone contributing and sharing information through the computerized communications network, the more responsive can the industry become to the demands of consumers and to the needs of society.

Examples of successful producer cooperatives are rare, because access to the capital needed to set them up is restricted by private ownership, by banks and state controls. However, the Mondragon cooperative in the Basque region of northern Spain is a celebrated example that comprises about a hundred industrial enterprises, a bank, shops, schools and a college. Each enterprise is run by the worker-owners, who are the shareholders and who have one vote each, not, as in most shareholders' meetings, votes in proportion to capital invested. Workers' councils elect an executive, which in turn chooses the managers, who can speak but not vote at council.

New technology extends opportunities for sharing information and decision-making beyond producer associations to the whole society. The basis for informed democracy is just that: information. Education is the single most important investment in the knowledge industry that is supposed to be shifting the economy of the developed world from an industrial to an information base. Professor Tom Stonier of Bradford University's Department of Science and Society has calculated the costs of providing all children in Britain with a computer system to be used at home and at school. He reckoned that

> £200 per personal system should buy a lot. It should include a small portable keyboard which could be carried back and forth the way one carries books. A modem at home to plug into the telephone system and similar drives at school. Disc drives, printing facilities for home and school, and other peripherals in schools ranging from remote-controlled turtles and other robots, sophisticated software, hard-disc back-up and expert system facilities. If spread over a six-year period would run to approximately £500 million a year or 5 per cent of the present education budget. As a result, the country would become truly computerate, for you would be getting such equipment into the majority of homes. The amount of commercial activity generated in terms of hardware and software production, servicing, training, etc., would provide a further instructive stimulus to the economy and create the kind of intellectual infrastructure to assure a technologically literate society in the next century.
> (Quoted in Ainley, 1990b, p. 120)

Yet a redirection of resources to enable schools to give all their pupils the pre-vocational skills necessary for full computer literacy would still provide only the technical potential to create a new and unified system of vocational education and training. A new curriculum to facilitate transfer between its different levels is also required. Nor could the process of creating an informed society be limited to the schools and colleges alone. The mass media and advertising would have a vital role to play. Indeed, it has been seen that with accelerating social change, and in order to utilize new technology to its fullest potential, as in Hirschhorn's factory of the future, education can no longer be restricted to educational institutions but must be recognized as lifelong learning. This is now so generally accepted as to be a cliché, yet its implications have hardly begun to be grasped. Indeed, 'The challenge of ever implementing that proposal would be formidable, less for its cost than its contradiction of deeply grooved hierarchies of "the educated", "the trained" and "the workers" ' (Professor Tony Edwards, 1983, quoted in Ainley, 1990a).

Faced with the new possibilities opened up by new technology, there seems an almost deliberate but unconscious and, as it were, instinctive reaction by the state. Dedicated to preserving the power of those who profit directly from the destructive commodity cycle, this reaction takes the form of redoubling obsessive secrecy and closing down and limiting people's educational experiences. Instead of the application of communications technology at every level of learning to allow imagination free rein to develop from experience the new ideas necessary to comprehend and deal with rapidly changing reality, there seems a desperate rearguard action to push the new conceptions formed from new interconnections back into obsolete subject discipline boxes, as in the so-called 'national' curriculum for schools. While this curriculum may have had the incidental benefit of encouraging scientific study in early-years schooling, its traditional subject discipline approach, modelled on the 1903 grammar school curriculum, goes against the grain of recent scientific discovery. For at present there is a ferment of new scientific knowledge as communications are speeded up and barriers between formerly discrete academic disciplines crumble. Nor does a uniform 'national' approach allow these new ideas to be developed generally or applied practically in local project based work. Similar objections could be raised to the latest proposals for higher education, which, while they might increase access (though they are hardly likely to do so when coupled with the introduction of student loans to pay for full-cost fees), will at the same time separate teaching from research. Instead, what is required is that all students should have opportunities for independent study so as to contribute to genuine scientific discovery or original artistic creation as a part of their courses (see Robbins, 1988).

In fact, recent education policy demonstrates very clearly the alternative use to which new technology can be put to sustain an ignorant rather than an informed society. In the process uncertain and indefinable qualities are being degraded to numerically exact quantities for insertion and sale in the commodity-for-profit cycle. Social goals for education, like increasing equality and opportunity, have been replaced by the financial accounting of efficiency and value for money. Services, like education, can then be 'costed' and 'compared' by their users, redefined as 'customers', especially if their infinite and unpredictable possibilities can be contained within narrow enough specifications of 'outputs'. From this comes the current obsession with spelling, which is of limited educational relevance but can be measured easily in the simple tests allowing parents to compare schools in the marketplace being constructed within the framework of the 1988 Act. The market concept of education contained within this legislation may be new for schools and colleges but it has been replicated throughout the public services.

The moves towards a public service market, while they give consumers 'rights' over the services they use, have notably involved a loss of the democratic rights of accountability and public control over the providers of local services – the district and metropolitan authorities. The latter have been abolished, while the former have had their role recast by central government legislation, from being responsible to their local electorates towards becoming boards of managing directors seeking tenders, issuing contracts and monitoring the performance of separate subcontractors. The moves towards so-called 'enabling' local authorities, endorsed by all three main electoral parties, mirror the 'quangoizing' or 'franchising' that has occurred in the central state, again with a parallel loss of accountability and democratic control. There the vestiges of democratic representation that remain are also becoming commodified, as parties and personalities are packaged and sold in elections increasingly open to media manipulation. Telecommunications that are used only to provide home-based shopping and entertainments for homebound consumers contribute to this privatization and consumerization of social life.

Consumer choice between the range of goods on offer in the marketplace is being confused with democratic determination of what needs to be produced for whom and why, at what cost to its producers and to the environment. Free-market philosophies advocate consumer accountability as the most efficient method of public accountability, substituting 'quality control' for democracy. The logic of this argument, which justifies the marketing of public services, is that a 'free market' is more democratic than any form of democracy. Free markets are thus the essence of and have primacy over democracy, as once stated by Sir Keith Joseph. According to such arguments, vast multinational bureaucratic corporations do not need to be made democratically accountable, save to their majority shareholders, for the decisions they inflict upon, literally, billions of people, because they have been endorsed by the mandate of the market. Local councils, education and health authorities, on the other hand, have to be made 'more accountable' and less democratic, by converting their services into commodities that can be quantified so as to compete in the open market of 'free' consumer choice. This consumerization of social life is also a form of modernization and represents a new sort of 'mixed' economy in which, as former state services are privatized, the state also increasingly subsidizes what are regarded as profitable private investments. This is the form of modernization that was chosen, or was fortuitously stumbled upon, by the Thatcher governments of the 1980s. But, rather than offering a way out of the intractable social and cultural malaise that was the legacy of Britain's industrial primacy and imperial past, this moribund market modernization led only to increasing fragmentation between individual consumers and built upon and heightened existing cultural differences between social groups.

CULTURAL DIFFERENCES, ECONOMIC SIMILARITY

Pierre Bourdieu, who is undoubtedly the most significant sociologist of education since Durkheim, developed what he called 'a general anthropology of power and legitimacy' that helps to explain the system of cultural differences between groups and individuals developed from the past by modern consumerism. It is an important principle of his explanation that the marks of social classification are 'culturally arbitrary' but that they nevertheless inflict 'symbolic violence' upon those who are unable to acquire the 'cultural capital' needed to maintain or advance their position from the base of the social hierarchy. Cultural capital is not necessarily the same as material wealth, however, just as the fabulous riches of a pop star or footballer do not automatically catapult them into the employing class and, to keep the credibility that helps to generate their income, may even require that they remain in contact with their working-class origins. Money cannot buy class, as they say. (Actually it can, but usually it takes two generations to do so, as the pioneer industrialists of the nineteenth century found. They expensively educated their sons so that they could acceptably marry into the aristocracy. They thus saved that social anachronism from extinction, but with the loss of their children, who declined ever again to soil their hands with practical trades and manufacture. Such at least is one influential version of the history of England's debilitating weakness for valuing the practice of effete arts over the wealth necessary to sustain them.)

In his *Anatomy of Taste*, Bourdieu (1976) diagrammatically disentangled the distinction between cultural and material capital, both of which may be more or less directly inherited or acquired. As described by his English interpreter and translator, Derek Robbins, he superimposed

> a map of the social space of life-styles over a corresponding map of the space of social positions by means of transparent, flimsy paper. Each page is organised to present a high volume of capital at the top of the page and a low volume at the bottom; and to the left represents high cultural capital whereas to the right represents high economic capital. Looking through the flimsy paper it is, for instance, possible to read a series of correspondences. The life-style corresponding with the farmers at the bottom of the centre of the page, with an income of 13,000 francs, includes football and the consumption of ordinary red wine; whereas the life-style corresponding with the liberal professions at the top of the centre of the page, with an income of 83,000 francs, includes golf and whisky. To the top left where higher education teachers are situated (possessing, that is, a high volume of capital of a cultural kind), a typical life-style correspondence is the music of Boulez, whereas at an equivalent level on the top right where industrialists and commercial employers are situated (possessing, that is, economic capital), a typical life-style correspondence is, comparably, the Hungarian Rhapsody. In order to try to indicate the temporal dimension, Bourdieu suggests, with an arrow, a declining, rising, or static social trajectory for each of the groups situated in the map of social positions.
>
> (Robbins, 1991, p. 126)

As well as clarifying the difference between class of origin and class of destination, Bourdieu's representation removes many of the conceptual confusions into which sociology has talked itself by reifying class in terms of status, instead of viewing class essentially as a power relationship. This is because the definition of class that English sociology predominantly adopted was either the Registrar General's five-class schema, originally elaborated by civil servants in 1911 for a comparative study of infant mortality, or the more recent refinement of it by Moser and Hall in 1954. This graded hierarchy ranked the skill levels of different occupations according to the estimation of those drawing it up, their own function thereby figuring at a higher level than it might otherwise have done. In addition, there was a tendency for the upper or ruling classes to disappear from the taxonomy – perhaps because they tend not to have any very precisely defined occupation! These measures of statistical estimations of the social status of various occupations were also assumed to be static and unchanging indicators of a settled social situation, rather than subject to increasingly rapid economic and technological transformation. As reality caught up with sociological models, earnest debate in the profession's journal *Sociology* questioned whether no, two, three, five or seven classes now exist in the UK. The logical step of abandoning class as a classificatory device was taken by many, including those preferring for statistical applications a sliding scale of infinite gradation of 'Social Stratification and Occupations', known as the Cambridge scale (see Stewart *et al.*, 1980). This sort of sampling device is facilitated by the sophisticated computer packages now available for analysing the large-scale data-sets made available by the application of new technology, and to which sociological investigation increasingly tends to be limited.

The influential English sociologist Ray Pahl (1989, p. 710) is representative in arguing that class might have been a useful conceptual tool in the nineteenth century when disparities between rich and poor were so much greater, but that these extremes have now been overcome. Ownership then, he and others argued, was concentrated in few hands but is now dispersed among institutions in which there are many investors rather than individual capitalists. Similarly, the concentration of productive labourers in factories has been succeeded by disparate and diverse employees in offices and services. His arguments are identical to those recently repeated by the advocates of a new post-modern, post-Fordist stage of development but familiar as Bell's post-industrial society (see p. 3). In this new society, consumption assumes a centrality over the productive work of the past. In addition, the inability of the old conceptions of social class to include women, other than as appendages to their husbands or fathers, has made the assertion of classlessness and the advocacy in its place of a society of competing interest groups, following Weber rather than Marx, attractive to some feminist sociologists. However, it was Rosemary Crompton, a feminist sociologist adhering to a class analysis, who in her criticism of Pahl's position asserted that 'The way ahead for social scientists is to stop arguing about whether or not "class analysis" has lost its utility but to recognise the varied meanings of the concept' (Crompton, 1991, p. 113).

This is what is being argued here. The collapse of the old, tripartite class world has been succeeded by a new appearance of pluralism, where no one is sure any longer of the present meaning of the previously commonly understood terms 'working class' and 'middle class'. This has taken place in the context of a cultural change that has emphasized individual judgement to negotiate roles following personal preference. The previously well-defined social situation is becoming, as Roberts and his colleagues recorded of their 1972 survey in Liverpool, for both the traditional working and middle classes on either side of the conventional manual–non-manual divide, the 'fragmentary class structure' (Roberts et al., 1977). In radio, Jackson's (1964) symbolic distinctions between the Light Programme, the Home Service and the Third Programme have been replaced by a plethora of competing local and national stations, each catering to particular tastes in jazz, soul, rap, reggae, bhangra and even 'golden oldies', 'easy listening' and classical music, as well as sports, talk and news channels. Commercial divisions between overlapping markets for different ages, genders and races have thus supplanted the BBC's former paternalistic provision for three classes.

Just because the meaning of terms in popular understanding has changed, it does not mean that the traditional sociological discriminations have totally lost their utility, even if they now have little correspondence with the conceptions of class held by those to whom the definitions are applied. In any case, sociology's answer, when confronted with the fact that most people do not see themselves as sociologists imagine them, is to reply that this does not matter. Since sociologists consider themselves as standing outside of or beyond the class system by virtue of their objective and more or less scientific understanding of it, they think that they know better than their subjects of study (rather as many Marxists still consider they possess a 'true consciousness' of class realities, even if the proletariat they aspire to lead is temporarily baffled by the wiles of capitalism into a 'false consciousness' of its real destiny). Although sociological measures of class are largely based upon official estimations of the social statuses of occupations and therefore reflect the traditional distinction between mental and manual labour, the erosion of which is at the root of the changes that have taken place, such measures may yet prove useful for describing certain social situations and for predicting supposedly significant behaviours from them. Typically these are voting intentions, given social ascription by class not only based upon occupation but supplemented by other indicators, such as income, occupation of male head of household, car and home ownership, or educational qualifications. (The latter are customarily taken by sociologists as a proxy for social status, since, among other things, this also tends to elevate their own situation.)

The division by socio-economic groups (SEGs) adopted by the Office of Population Censuses and Statistics in 1951 gives a very precise seventeen-point table running from (1) Employers and managers in central and local government, industry, commerce, etc. – large establishments, to (2) Employers and managers in industry, commerce, etc. – small establishments, through, familiarly, (9) Skilled manual workers, (10) Semi-skilled manual workers and (11) Unskilled manual workers, right down to (15) Agricultural workers, (16) Members of armed forces [*sic*] and (17) Inadequately described and not stated occupations. While they do not exactly correspond with the Registrar General's categories, the SEGs serve to order and classify the vast amounts of data obtained from census returns, and efforts are made to keep up to date with changes in the labour market. A substantial revision was undertaken in 1961 when, for example, postmen and telephone operators were demoted and airline pilots promoted a group.

Argument occurs about which SEG belongs in which class, as well as the numbers and names of the classes – principally an argument about the emergence since the war of a supposed 'new middle', sometimes 'new petit bourgeois', or, more generally, 'service' class. The most popular current scheme, the neo-Weberian Goldthorpe classification of 1980, distinguishes a service class, intermediate strata and working class. This not only once again dissolves the numerically insignificant but socially powerful ruling class in the service class but also reproduces the conventional manual–non-manual division as well as the traditional upper, middle and working trisection. The main sociological opposition to this typology comes from the Marxist approaches of, for example, Westergaard and Resler (1976), who dismissed 'middle class' as 'a misleading term'. (Not all Marxists, it should be pointed out, agree with them; for instance, the Trotskyist Socialist Workers' Party, which has taken over the old Communist Party mantle as the largest extra-parliamentary party on the British left, currently holds to an analysis that distinguishes a new middle or service class from the working class, though – unlike Goldthorpe – the SWP sees this new class as separate from the capitalist ruling class.) Permutations of the debate produce compromises such as Erik Wright's (1984) neo-Marxist notion of some statuses, such as higher-education students, having 'contradictory class locations' in which they share attributes of the classes above and below them and from which individuals may transfer either up or down the ladder.

Such conceptions are more or less useful for social analysis and prediction, just as the As, Bs and Cs of the advertising agencies and opinion polls with their various specialized refinements – C1s, C2s, Ds and Es – help the more accurate targeting and promotion of various commodities, including politicians and their policies, as in the 1992 general election when both main parties assiduously courted the C2s. Eating preferences, for example, may not be the most significant of human behaviours, yet they are predicted extremely well by this definition of social class: while the As and Bs sit down to *saumon en croute* (courtesy of Marks & Spencer), the CDEs eat fish and chips (courtesy of Jaconelli). What is interesting is whether such small behaviours are related to big behaviours that have wider consequences, but they do demonstrate that class so defined exists, if only in the (cultural) form of food demarcations. (I am indebted for this example to Sheena Ashford. The example, incidentally, also illustrates Bourdieu's principle of cultural arbitrariness in such matters of taste, for with over-fishing cod may become as rare as salmon once was, and salmon through fish-farming is becoming as common as cod used to be, so that the polarities may reverse, As and Bs preferring cod mornay and CDEs salmon and chips – only fancy French names and chips remaining constant! Once oysters were a food for poor people, though as they became scarcer they were no longer cooked in pies but savoured raw.)

Such cultural variations and the categorization of them along the A to E scale do not, however, necessarily correspond with how people think of themselves. Nor do people necessarily share the same understanding of the questions they are asked, by sociologists, advertising agents or opinion pollsters, as their questioners. As a result, which box a respondent will tick in a questionnaire does not necessarily coincide with what that same person will say in one interview as compared with another in different circumstances, nor with how he or she will behave in specific situations. This was clearly demonstrated by the opinion polls predicting Conservative defeat in the 1992 British general election. The lesson has been lost on most sociologists, who continue to base their researches upon questionnaires that are, in most cases, less well constructed than those of the pollsters.

It is a truism that, as Hutson and Jenkins (1989, p. 113) asserted, 'One's perception of the class structure is closely linked to one's position within it', but their speculation that 'The closer to the bottom of the hierarchies of class, status and power an individual is, the shorter the scale of those hierarchies is perceived to be. Conversely, the closer to the top a person is, the greater the perceived social and economic distance between top and bottom' raises a number of questions. (Perhaps it is misled by the implicit metaphor of a social pyramid, whereas the true representational shape of society is a diamond, lozenge or egg shape, tapering both at base and apex but considerably sharper towards what Swift's Gulliver called the 'smaller' rather than the 'big' end of the egg, in fact, so sharp it more nearly resembles a tear drop.) The speculation would, however, go some way towards explaining the paradox that Brown and Scase (1991) noted at the end of the 1980s, when 'the restructuring of class relations has increased material inequalities but reduced the level of subjective awareness of them' (p. 21).

The widening of differentials along a spectrum, the poles of which are growing further apart, may offer the illusion of equality, or at least of only minor quantitative variations, to those between the two extremes. Many people may agree with all the economic indicators that, since the mid-1970s, the rich have got richer and the poor poorer (for example, as recorded by Leadbeater (1989), the top 10 per cent were 80 per cent better off in 1985 than in 1979, while the bottom 10 per cent were 4 per cent worse off). Yet most see themselves as situated between these two opposites. Their position relative to others in the same intermediate position is also not fixed but grows more fluid with rapid changes in wages and employment status following the latest applications of new technology. This has led to the upsetting of many an applecart, as many formerly traditional working-class occupations are now materially more advanced than classically middle-class professionals on relatively lower wages. This is also nothing new, considering that Victorian clerks or elementary school teachers were never paid as much as skilled artisans. What is new is the rapidity and fluidity of these transformations.

Bourdieu's dual representation of material and cultural capital can help us to visualize a way out of these conundrums. Indeed, it can then be seen how popular perceptions of social status employ material definitions, in terms of income and the personal accumulation of commodities – from house, car and white goods ownership to holidays abroad – simultaneously with the cultural definitions of affiliation to more or less high or popular culture based mainly upon education. As Bourdieu also indicated, the signs of cultural distinction are arbitrary and constantly altered by those in a position to control the rules of the game, such as the arbiters of taste and fashion. At the same time individuals and groups, especially young people asserting an adult status in the existing hierarchy for the first time, construct their own identities, using such resources as are available to them, either to conform or to diverge from the predominant norms presented to them.

Cultural distinctions between classes are thus also age- and gender-specific and manifested in such items as the notorious English concern with accent, as well as in culturally inherited notions of clean and unclean, and taboos referring to touchstones like spitting, swearing and violence, as well as, more superficially, deportment, diet and dress. To add to the complications, as well as varying between genders and according to age, as Phil Cohen pointed out, 'each class culture throws its own grid of representation over the life cycle, [so that] what is a mark of maturity in one may be a sign of backwardness in another' (quoted in Ainley, 1991, p. 6). Violence is a good example of this, being regarded as childish by the middle class in situations where it would be seen as an appropriate last resort by many (male) workers and where failure so to respond would be seen as 'effeminate'. This relates again to the vexed question of language, for middle-class people can generally not only rely upon the forces of the law to uphold their interest in a situation without having resort to violence, but also have recourse to a large vocabulary of supposed reasonableness with which to talk their way out of difficulties. This does not mean, as some have asserted, that working-class language is somehow deficient, nor that resort to violence rather than reason, especially in child-rearing, is the source of authoritarian tendencies among the proletariat, rendering them susceptible to totalitarian politicians, as was seriously suggested by others. Labov (1973) discredited such notions by pointing to the logic of non-standard English. As he put it, 'Our work in the speech community makes it painfully obvious that in many ways working-class speakers are more effective narrators, reasoners and debaters than middle-class speakers who temporise, qualify, and lose their argument in a mass of irrelevant detail' (p. 34).

Labov's demonstration did little to deter Bernstein's elaborate construction of a theory of class codes of language use. He took his argument to its logical conclusion by proposing that the different conditions of the economic life of working and middle classes gave rise to different family structures, to different relations within the family and consequently to different types of language acquisition and use. The end-result of such differently codified uses of language, according to Bernstein, is complete non-communication between the patients and psychotherapists he was studying, who were typically members of different classes employing mutually incomprehensible codes of language (Bernstein, 1964, pp. 54–64). In short, logically but absurdly, they might as well have been speaking different languages; though it can be added that the cultural difference of actually speaking a different language is not sufficient to place a person in a different social class from another.

Sociological interviews with working-class subjects are typically carried out by interviewers who regard themselves, if not as middle class and therefore different from or superior to their interviewees, then as having a real or true perception of the situation that is denied to their unenlightened subjects. This does not mean they are talking different languages but it certainly often causes confusion. As a result, the appreciation of a similarity in class ascription behind apparently minor status differences may emerge in a detailed interview, whereas conventional class ascriptions ticked in a questionnaire are often affected by traditional notions. In addition, people's perceptions are heavily influenced by what Ashton et al. (1990, p. 193) called 'local labour market cultures'. These have special relevance not only in the regions but also for ethnic and national minorities. Above all, to situate oneself vaguely but comfortably in a 'homogenized centre', as it has been called, requires reference to significantly different others both above and below. Thus, for people who say, 'Well, I don't quite know what I am – but I'm definitely not one of *them*', class is an important and salient issue (another point made to me by Sheena Ashford). In a similar way, the traditional proletariat situated itself uncomfortably but defiantly at the base of the social mountain by reference to 'them' above. 'They' have indeed long remained the same, but in recent years it has been alleged that a new so-called 'underclass' has emerged as from under a rock at the bottom of society. In addition to the elision of the traditionally fundamental divide between manual and mental workers, it is perhaps the creation of this factor, whether in reality or only in appearance, that has contributed to the new perception of classlessness. Or rather, the supposed existence of a new underclass is an additional factor in the confused muddling of various notions of middle and working classness, of old and new material and cultural distinctions, in the new working middle of society.

THE RESURRECTION OF THE ROUGH

The poor have not always been with us. Of course, in any hierarchical society there is bound to be relative wealth and poverty. Relative poverty – the fact that many of the poorest people in the richest countries own television sets that would be envied by the wretched of the earth struggling for daily survival in the countries of the Third World – is not what is at issue. For any society a historically varying, but nevertheless at any one time absolute, level of deprivation can be set. As Townsend (1987, p. 100) concluded a long debate, 'if people cannot obtain, at all or sufficiently, the conditions of life – that is, the diets, amenities, standards and services – which allow them to play the roles, participate in the relationships and follow the customary behaviour which is expected of them by virtue of their membership of society; if they lack or are denied resources to obtain access to these conditions of life and so fulfil membership of society they may be said to be in poverty'. In a capitalist society, the defining feature of which is a free labour market, for the vast majority of the population individual access to the share of collective wealth necessary to sustain an independent existence and so 'fulfil membership of society' lies through earning wages. Those who are unable to do this, if only temporarily because they are too young, nursing parents, injured or ill, or permanently through infirmity or severe disability, need not necessarily be poor but they are dependent upon others to provide them with the means of life. Yet such ideological weight is placed upon the virtues of independence, connected as they are with core notions of freedom and individuality, that dependence is widely conceived of as shaming and places dependent people in an infantile relation to those they are dependent upon – 'unable to stand on their own two feet'.

Previously, within the traditional working class, a 'cycle of poverty' had regularly reduced older and disabled people, plus parents and children generally, to relative poverty. In addition since the end of the long boom in the decades after the Second World War, millions of people have been placed in such a situation of dependence upon the state by the return of mass unemployment. Rather than being a temporary and cyclical phenomenon, permanent mass unemployment is now accepted as a structural necessity for the continued functioning of the economic system. Indeed, the critical level of unemployment that is regarded as 'the trigger' to 'fuel inflation' has been steadily raised. It is no coincidence that with an army of the unemployed, varying in number between one and a half million, even during an upswing, and over three million in a downturn, observers have descried 'the making of a British underclass'.

Nick Mann (1991) began by observing that sociologists who have advanced the theory that there is a new class division in society separating 'the underclass' from the rest have been given publicity that is not usually granted to anyone claiming to prove the existence of class divisions in what is popularly presented as a society of equal opportunity. The most influential of these media-promoted pundits, the American Charles Murray, whose 1990 polemic *The Emerging British UNDERCLASS* was also featured in a special issue of *The Sunday Times* magazine (26 November 1989), having been sponsored in his research in Britain by Rupert Murdoch's News International. As Mann points out, this merely follows 'a long tradition of commentators who have observed a stratum of hopeless degenerates' at the bottom of society. The names for this section of society have varied down the years: 'excluded groups, marginalized groups, underclass, residuum, the poor, reserve army of labour, housing and social security classes, stagnant reserve army, relative surplus population and the lumpenproletariat are all terms that have been used to describe a layer within, or beneath, the working class' (p. 160). Mann even added his own contribution to the list – lapilli, meaning 'small fragments of lava ejected from a volcano' and, presumably, melting back into the molten flow when the temperature rises again. For, 'while each generation has seen a sub-stratum within the working class, each period has also witnessed the rehabilitation of that sub-stratum. The Victorian residuum appears to have evaporated in the heat of the First World War. Likewise, the class of unemployables of the inter-war period failed to survive the Second World War' (p. 107). Where, asked Mann, did this leave the theory that the underclass reproduced itself through a culture of poverty transmitted down the generations?

The reintroduction of the term 'underclass' to Britain from its latest semi-racist incarnation in the United States can be traced to Sir Keith Joseph, as he then was. While Minister for Health and Social Services in Heath's government, he made a number of speeches claiming that a 'cycle of deprivation' created by dependency upon the state trapped families in poverty. Joseph, it should be recalled, became Mrs Thatcher's *éminence grise* after sponsoring the new leader against Heath. Following the assassination of Airey Neave, Joseph was the chief influence over Thatcher until his own departure from the scene, 'like a general after a catastrophic defeat', as Paul Johnson, one of his admirers, wrote at the time (*TES*, 11 April 1986). As Mrs Thatcher acknowledged in her letter answering his resignation, Joseph 'more than anyone else was the architect who shaped the policies which led to victory in two [later three] elections'. Contrary to the advice even of his own monetarist mentor Hayek, who doubted that any democratic government could survive for more than two or three years with an unemployment level over 10 per cent, Sir Keith had persisted in his belief that times had changed since the 1930s. The lesson that he drew from Heath's defeat by the miners was that it had been wrong to abandon the policy of confrontation and rising unemployment associated with Heath's brief Selsdon-man phase. In opposition he concluded that unemployment could have been allowed to rise far beyond the half million it had reached by 1972 until it found its 'natural' level and cleared the market. Unlike the Labour government that replaced

Heath, Joseph accepted that high unemployment was a permanent and structural necessity and not a temporary and cyclical phenomenon that would disappear with economic upturn. Times had changed, he argued, so that hunger marches and rioting would not be the automatic response to the high levels of unemployment he saw as essential to what he called 'a law-abiding free enterprise reconstruction of Britain's social relations of production' (see Ainley and Corney, 1990, p. 46).

Joseph had at first recommended compulsory sterilization for those 'doomed to an uphill struggle against the disadvantages of a deprived family background' so that they would not themselves become 'in their turn the parents of deprived families', but was forced to recant by the ensuing outcry. Unusually, Joseph's eugenicist ideas had not included a racial element – he saw the congenitally incapable, for whom he also suggested a narrowly vocational schooling, as evenly spread across all racial groups. Nevertheless, a racist tinge was never far from the policies of successive Conservative governments, first spelled out by Mrs Thatcher in a television interview in 1978 when she said that 'People [by which she meant white people] are really rather afraid that this country might be swamped by people with a different culture' (by which she meant black people). So impressed were Tory Party tacticians by the 11 per cent lead this remark immediately produced in the opinion polls that they had her repeat it two weeks before the 1979 election when it rather looked as if she might lose. In government this concern with those whom the sole surviving Tory grandee, William Whitelaw, used to call 'our people' continued right through to the way in which Mrs Thatcher's chosen successor conducted the pre-election negotiations on European unity as a referendum on national sovereignty, urged on by a tabloid press campaign threatening waves of uncontrolled immigration from the Continent. Indeed, throughout the period immigration policy, defining black and Asian people as a problem, has been central to the new definition of nationhood with which adherence to the new enterprise state has been sustained.

Permanent, long-term, structural unemployment has posed new problems of legitimacy for the state. This problem was made more acute by the fact that the doubling of unemployment from one and a half to three million, which was the immediate labour market response to the monetarist economic policies unleashed after 1979, particularly affected young people and coincided with a demographic boom in the numbers of school-leavers. As Ashton *et al.* (1990) concluded their authoritative study, *Restructuring the Labour Market*, looking particularly at the implications for youth: 'Since our research began in the late 1970s, there has been a progressive transformation of the lower segments of the labour market as they have become dominated by insecure, casual, temporary and part-time jobs. As a result, the problem of unemployment is itself becoming transformed and incorporated into the everyday experience of a large section of the working class' (p. 203). Moreover, as Offe wrote in 1985, 'For the foreseeable future labour markets in many countries will continue to exhibit a declining absorption potential, thus removing or excluding increasing numbers of potential workers [and] separating the employed and the non-employed' (p. 3).

The government's initial answer to this crisis of legitimacy for the belief in equality of opportunity, supposedly provided to all by education but denied to many by the realities of the labour market, was a policy of vocationalism which they inherited from Labour. Thus, Joseph's policy while he was Minister of Education was to provide two types of schooling that would separate the vocational goats from the academic sheep. His concern was always with a vocational schooling for the majority of school-leavers, who were intended to pass via youth training into the flexible, semi-skilled and low-wage labour force with which the government intended Britain to compete with the rest of the world. For this reason Joseph opposed the 1988 Education Act, which he saw as reverting to an outdated and inappropriate academicism for all school students and encouraging a competition between schools which the majority of pupils were bound to lose.

An alternative to the tripartite divisions of the past for a labour market that lacks the skilled manual work any longer to sustain them, to vocational sorting for semi-skilled, insecure employment, or to unequal competition for academic access to a secure, managerial and administrative core, is to sustain an 'underclass'. This acts as a spur to the majority who seek to maintain their independence at all costs so as to avoid relegation to dependence upon the reduced services of the state. This was the reality of the 'property-owning democracy' Mrs Thatcher sought to create. Defined against it was a modern version of the nineteenth-century 'people of no property'. Reduced from a majority to a minority, this group was still sizeable enough to threaten, if not the whole of society as in the past, then at least many millions of dutifully employed, desperately mortgage-paying and indebted citizens striving to rise above it and prepared to vote Conservative in the hope of doing so. For increasingly this was how the new division in society was coming to be defined – by intermittent and unskilled employment, dependence upon state benefits, council house ownership and the overseeing of personal affairs by social workers and the police, especially for 'problem' families stigmatized and segregated on to special estates, and by lack of enterprise to invest in what, with the aetiolation of public services, have become the necessities for independent existence – private or occupational pensions and health care, private education, home and car ownership.

While this new state of affairs moves society towards the widely predicted 'two-thirds, one-third' division, it also uncannily reproduces the same distinctions between deserving and undeserving claimants that have haunted the discussion and administration of welfare since the introduction of the New Poor Law in 1834, i.e. since the extension of a free labour market to the entire population (see Polanyi, 1946). Indeed, the 1988 social security legislation followed an extensive review, which stated as its aim the need to retarget benefits to 'those most in need', who in the past would have been called 'the working poor', particularly those with children. Meanwhile the rest, known formerly as the idle but able-bodied poor, were to be set to work to earn their maintenance on publicly provided benefits. Entitlements to benefits for many claimants and for many items for which they were previously entitled to claim have been replaced by discretion and are no longer grants but loans. The role played by charity is widened to narrow the state role here as elsewhere. Charity is by its nature demeaning for those who receive it not as a right but by discretion, and serves to heighten the contrast with the enterprise and independence of those who are in a position but not under an obligation to give it. For the ordinary taxpayers of whom charity is demanded, unlike the celebrities and companies who give it in order to advertise themselves or their wares, numberless charities arising from incessant emergencies increasingly fill the gaps in supposedly statutory provision, as basic state services like health and education are delivered by the short-term contract culture of the new enterprise state.

Not only these familiar features of Victoriana but also past popular reflections reconstitute the official distinctions between deserving and undeserving objects of charity, amplified by what Mann called the 'scroungermania' of the mass media. The place of the Victorian Irish navvy as the traditional stereotype of the 'rough' has been taken by the supposedly culturally alien and visibly identifiable black 'immigrant'. Thus earlier anti-Catholic prejudice in the one case and imperial disdain for the formerly enslaved and 'uncivilized' former colonial populations in the other have served to shore up the image of the respectable working man whose efforts to carve out for himself an independent place in the world are besieged on all sides by invading armies of the unskilled prepared to undercut the wages he has fought so hard to maintain and raise. The position of the Asians in this white demonology also reproduces that of the stereotyped Jews of Victorian and earlier times, all of whom, notwithstanding visible evidence to the contrary, supposedly lived upon the sweat of the working man.

The new racialization of the resurrected division between the respectable and the rough is of course undercut by two factors: on the one hand, not all black and Asian people can be characterized as belonging to 'the underclass'. Although this is the predominant stereotype conveyed by the mass media, there is a small but significant and growing black middle class in the old sense of non-manual and professional employment (see Daye, 1989). Beyond the much smaller numbers of wealthy black and Asian business people and the large petty bourgeoisie of small shopkeepers, the proportion of skilled workers in the older generation of West Indians, particularly, has always been higher than for the whole population. On the other hand, the attempt made in the late 1970s by the police to criminalize all black youth (see CCCS, 1982) would be rendered less easy today by the existence of whole districts and regions where permanent unemployment has afflicted two generations of white as well as black workers. For 'poor whites' in similar circumstances in the southern United States, Australia, South Africa and other countries, it has long been a standard response to their situation, often sustained or encouraged by government, to assert their continued sense of belonging and to deny their actual exclusion by identifying with the dominant white powerholders against formerly subservient 'aliens' with whom they are forced to compete for dwindling resources, especially jobs and houses. The incipient fascism of this response is today underlined by a growing international dimension. As Amin wrote in 1989, 'If the present road of development continues, the North–South contradiction will inevitably become more and more explosive, thereby engendering, among other things, an intensified racism in the countries of developed capitalism, of which the prejudice against the Third World is only a precursor . . . In this sense, Nazism, far from being an aberration, always remains a latent possibility' (pp. 148, 114).

If this possibility is to be avoided, the excluded minority, black and white, must be reintegrated into society by a return to full employment and the division that has been created between a supposedly inferior and dependent 'underclass' and the majority of independent and respectable citizens must be overcome. Two factors provide a historical opportunity for this possibility to be realized: one is the potential use that can be made of new technology to increase communication and extend democracy; the other is the gathering ecological crisis, which renders this increased cohesion and cooperation within society necessary for survival. However, before I examine these possibilities it is necessary to appreciate the effects that the ideological and material construction of a new 'underclass' have had upon the consciousness of those in the new middle of society.

Chapter 5

Popular Perceptions of Social Class

In ony country in the world, who are the only folk that ken whit it's like tae leeve in that country? The folk at the boattam. The rest can a' kid themselves oan. They can afford to hiv fancy ideas.

(Hugh McIlvanney, Docherty)

IN THE MIDDLE - BETWEEN THE SNOBS AND THE YOBS

In November 1990 the attention of the leading English Conservative newspaper, *The Daily Telegraph*, was momentarily diverted from the drama at Downing Street while, as the paper commented, 'MPs considered whether to elevate Mr Major, the son of a circus artist, to the nation's highest office.' In a widely reported case of appeal to the High Court, the *Telegraph* recorded the verdict of the Appeal Judge, Mr Justice Harman, 'whose top drawer credentials - Eton and the Coldstream Guards - are scarcely in doubt'. Harman ruled against a previous judgment in favour of Tory-controlled Westminster City Council, led by Lady Porter, daughter of an East End barrow-boy who founded the Tesco supermarket empire. The earlier judgment had invalidated a lease leaving the majority of the flats on a London housing estate 'as dwellings for the working classes within the meaning of the Housing Act 1925'. 'The fact that Parliament no longer used the term "working class" in housing legislation does not determine the meaning of those words in ordinary English speech,' declared the judge. 'The *Oxford English Dictionary*', to which he referred for his definition of meaning in ordinary speech, 'did not describe the term "working class" as obsolete, but defined it as "those employed to work for wages in manual or industrial occupations".' In a further twist to delight *Telegraph* readers, confirming their prejudices that class no longer had the social force that it used to have but was merely the source of amusing anecdotes such as this one, the paper added that the ruling was in favour of the owner of the estate, the sixth Duke of Westminster, reputedly Britain's wealthiest man.

Such ambiguity is a source of humour to those in the comfortable middle of society. The *Sunday Correspondent*, for example - itself, as a self-styled 'quality tabloid', pointing to an attempt to find common cultural ground in the material middle of society, though one that, also revealingly perhaps, did not long survive - announced a competition for its readers to provide a definition of 'working class'. The winner was: 'Wearing overalls on weekdays, painting someone else's house to earn money? You're working class. Wearing overalls at weekends, painting your own house to save money? You're middle class' (14 October 1990). If this definition played upon material similarities, the comedian Jasper Carrott's ferocious lampooning of *The Sun* and its readers accentuated cultural differences; for example, '*Financial Times* readers rule the country, while *Guardian* readers wished they ruled the country and *Sun* readers don't care who rules the country.'

Certainly, class as it was experienced and understood at the beginning of the century in the Western industrialized nations now has little more than an affective reality. What Sartre called 'the proletarian countenance with its violent oppositions, its great uniform and desert masses, its zones of shadow and its shores of light, the simple and urgent needs which illuminate it', has gone with the classical working class that brought it into existence. So, 'The simple, well-marked oppositions of the "proletarian" universe' have been replaced by 'the innumerable interwoven nuances of the "bourgeois" world' (Sartre, 1969, pp. 513, 514). The resulting 'fragmentary class structure', as Roberts and his fellow investigators called it in 1972, was a consequence of the economic and technical shifts in employment that have been described. It was also the outcome of a more or less conscious and continuous battle of ideas waged contemporaneously with political struggles on behalf of the ruling class by what Marxists call the ideological state apparatus (and not only the state, it could be added, given the influence of the privately owned press) to maintain 'ideological hegemony' over the subordinate classes in society.

Thus, in a period like the present in which the reality and the apprehension of social class are changing, as has been suggested, different and sometimes mutually contradictory conceptions can coexist, especially in the unformulated and spontaneous popular consciousness that is misleadingly called 'public opinion'. For the supposedly uniform 'public' with its 'common sense' and 'responsible opinion' is actually manufactured from all the various individuals and groups that collectively constitute society. As far as class is concerned, there are salient variations, both within the various classes, however defined, and by region, age, gender, nationality, ethnic grouping, etc.

In a period of accelerating social change, variation by age is especially significant as each generation apprehends the different reality into which it is born in a new way. There is thus what can be called a time lag in the mental maps of the world constructed by succeeding generations, themselves, in so far as they are accurate representations, always lagging behind changing reality itself. This is not to ignore the fact of continuing socialization as the perceptions of the younger generations tend towards those of the older. However, even the most obdurate functionalists cannot deny (though they cannot explain) that socialization does not reproduce social consciousness unaltered through time. There is a dialectic between the generations, which is heightened by rapid social change.

For those born and brought up in the old tripartite class world, including most middle-aged professional sociologists, traditional class concepts retain their reality. Yet these same lecturers, professors, etc. often find it hard to convey that reality to their students, who for the most part were born in a period when the erosion of the manual/ mental divide was undermining the previously clearly understood distinctions that to them now appear academic. Even if they appreciate the continuing usefulness of class measures for limited description and prediction, young people generally have a different perception of their social reality from that of their elders. To an extent this has always been the case in a changing society and it does not necessarily mean that in recent years young people have been 'duped by Thatcherism', as alleged by sociologists from the University of Essex studying the Youth Training Scheme. Most of their sample of youth trainees in Colchester at the end of the 1980s rejected the notion of social class, 'some flatly refusing to respond [to the question] because the idea smacked of snobbery, divisiveness and unequal worth'. As Lee *et al.* (1990) reported, their most common self-definition was middle class, 'by which they seemed to mean the bulk of ordinary people who lay between a small and remote upper class and a disreputable but diminishing lower class' (p. 126). This perception was not, as Lee and his colleagues implied it was, necessarily a 'false consciousness' masking the reality of a marginalized economic status for which youth training was preparing the young people. Nor was it only the consequence of ideological projections, either by themselves or by the ruling party in the state. It was also a reflection of a changed reality interpreted in a new way through both new and old ideas about social class.

Compared with young people's perceptions, the latest results from the largest and most representative sample of public opinion regularly conducted by the respected Social and Community Planning Research organization and reported in the *British Sociological Association Sourcebook 1983-89* showed that over all generations traditional class ascriptions held up remarkably consistently throughout the 1980s. People were shown a card and asked to read the suggestion on it that 'Most people see themselves as belonging to a particular social class', with the invitation to pick one of 'upper middle class, middle class, upper working class, working class, poor'. The percentage placing themselves in the combined working-class categories declined only from 67.8 per cent in 1983 to 65.5 per cent in 1989. There was no breakdown by age but another large and similarly representative sample of 16-19-year-olds who came of age in the 1980s in four contrasted areas showed that, when asked in questionnaires to assign themselves to one of three classes with 'don't know' and 'no class' as further options, 64 per cent of all those choosing one of the three class options called themselves working class as against 34 per cent middle class. As would be expected in a sample restricted to state school-leavers, numbers picking the third class option – upper middle class – were very low (less than 2 per cent). Four out of five respondents acknowledged social class, with Scots (or rather those from the Kirkcaldy district of Fife) being most likely not to put themselves in any social class. Residents of Swindon, a 'new town' in the then relatively prosperous south of England where processes of 'class disalignment' had supposedly gone furthest and more of the youngsters worked in offices, services and new-technology companies, were the most likely to call themselves middle class (39 per cent). This compared with the traditionally northern Liverpool, where more people were manually employed than elsewhere and where 60 per cent of respondents placed themselves in the working class. Despite there being many more women overall in 'non-manual' employment, young men and women in all areas were equally likely to assign themselves to the middle class, except in Swindon where fewer females did so. In the sample altogether, 79 per cent of school-leavers were in non-manual occupations yet 56 per cent of them called themselves working class. Since out of the 21 per cent in manual occupations, 56 per cent also called themselves working class, being in manual or non-manual employment made no difference to class affiliation. Nor did their class of origin have much effect: there was as little relation between self-assigned class and father's occupation as between self-assigned class and own occupation.

What did make a difference was area. More white-collar workers in Swindon than elsewhere rejected class categorization, and Swindon manual workers were least likely to call themselves working class: only just over half did so, compared with 83 per cent of

Liverpudlian manual workers. It is obvious therefore that perceptions of class structure vary widely by locality and that the sociological definition of class, which follows conventional distinctions between manual and non-manual work, bears little resemblance to the idea of class held by those to whom the definition was applied. This became even more apparent when forty young people were repeatedly interviewed in Liverpool over a period of three years, to ask them why they gave the questionnaire answers that they did. Their answers show once again that which box people tick on questionnaires is often not the same as what they say in the different circumstances of an interview. They also show that interviewees and respondents to questionnaires do not necessarily share the same understanding of the questions as their questioners. For many of the young people interviewed, 'middle class' was not different from 'working class'. Both of them, as a number of replies put it, have to work to live. Rather, 'middle' was seen by them as intermediate between rich and poor. So, 'I'm just ordinary – not posh and not scruffy.' However, while many youngsters defined themselves as being 'in the middle' between 'snobs' above and 'scallies' below, very few admitted in interview to being in the disreputable scallywag class. 'I'd like to be working class if I could get a job' or 'I'm not working so I'm not working class' were the nearest some interviewees came to placing themselves in this underclass of the new rough, who were used by many others as a reference point to put themselves in the respectably safe middle.

If there were an underclass of the new rough, its members would be the hardest to trace even in a large sample. However, if any such underclass existed anywhere, with its own distinctive pattern of life totally removed from any involvement in orthodox paid labour, it would surely be apparent in the continuously depressed economy of Merseyside. Yet even here, Roberts (1990) concluded, there was no evidence for the emergence of such an underclass that would remain unemployed if by some miracle full employment returned tomorrow. Sure enough, in the Liverpool young people's interview answers, while many agreed that the rich have got richer and the poor poorer, most saw themselves situated between these two diverging poles and none would directly identify themselves with either of them. While it is common for people to place themselves safely and non-committally 'in the middle', it is surely significant that the only apparent and unabashed representative of the underclass in the similarly economically depressed and geographically isolated Glasgow (advertising campaign face-lifts and superficial architectural refurbishments notwithstanding) is a fictional television stereotype, Rab C. Nesbitt, whose proud boast is that he is 'social scum'!

As suggested, the widening of differentials along a spectrum may even offer an illusion of equality to those 'in the middle', or at least of only minor quantitative variations separating those between the two extremes. Class then becomes, as one young man interviewed in Sheffield put it, 'a superficial thing – just how you talk and the clothes you wear'. The appreciation of a similarity behind apparently minor differences may then emerge in interview, whereas conventional class ascriptions ticked on a questionnaire are influenced by local labour market cultures. This affords an explanation of the resonance that Mr Major's proclamation of a 'classless society' initially found in many sections of the population. The notion had been rejected when it was previously enunciated in the tortured strains of Mrs Thatcher's acquired elocution and was subsequently overworked in the phoney notion of 'citizenship' defined in the limited terms of consumer rights (see p. 76). However, for a time the seemingly ridiculous idea that Thatcherism had arrived at its own utopia of a society of equally competing and achieving individuals did enjoy some public credibility. Given the redistribution of wealth that had actually taken place from the poorest to the wealthiest during the period, this was an extraordinary ideological assertion, even though it was supported, in large part, by the compliantly echoing mass media.

It has been suggested that the new class relations consequent upon the breakdown of the tripartite class system offer the basis for just such an ideological construction, but defined – despite the limitations and contradictions of this definition – in terms of nationality and race. This elides the real distinction between the two main classes in the national state of employers and employees, and creates an illusory division between them and the unemployed, who are stigmatized as inferior not only by poverty in material consumption and culturally arbitrary disadvantage, but also by unrespectable dependence upon the state. However, this is only one side of the latest ideological battle being waged over the popular perception of the future shape of society. On the other side, the new class alignment offers the opportunity of overcoming artificial cultural divisions and material inequalities sustained by the state in the interest of a real unity of working people, defined in the broadest and most classical sense of those who have to sell their labour to live, whether they are employed or unemployed, against those who live by buying it. This new and as yet inchoate conception of class places those whose interest lies in a future for themselves and their children in opposition to the small minority whose immediate personal gain dictates their functions as representatives of the power of money in a closed system of production for profit, which is rapidly and literally ruining all possibility for any human future.

It is this sense of a new working class that comes across in sentiments such as those of a Radio London phone-in caller on the subject, who defined as working class 'those who have to get up of a morning to go to work' as against those who – however hard they 'work' to maintain and multiply their wealth – are not compelled to do that work in order to live but could live without working from their unearned assets. In essence, the difference is between those who have to work for their money and those whose money works for them. It is true that many outside the employing or ruling class are functionaries of private or state capital who have amassed considerable sums and have investments sufficient to live on for some time before they find themselves, in Marx's words, 'on the pavement', and that private pensioners in particular are a notable source of support for the status quo from the so-called 'service class'. But this is where the illusive distinction lies between those, however occupied, who will never have to sell their own labour but can live exclusively and indefinitely upon the unearned labour of others, and those – variously and misleadingly called the new middle class, the service class, etc. – whose limited capital will run out, usually sooner rather than later, and who will therefore be forced again to join the labour market in seeking to sell their labour for the means to live along with the vast majority of their fellows.

The illusion that, in material terms, owning a larger house together with a few stocks and shares, or having an arbitrary cultural 'superiority' derived from education, distinguishes you from all the other sellers in the labour market is the source of a double use of the term 'snob' in the Liverpool interviews referred to above. 'Snob' was habitually used by the young people questioned in the traditional sense of the Victorian 'toff', as a synonym for ruling class. However, the word also had another sense when applied to someone who was not in the ruling class of employers but was actually a member of the working middle class, 'not posh and not scruffy', and who, like everyone else, had to work to live but who, unlike everyone else, thought of himself or herself as 'better than' or 'different from' the rest of working humanity. This is also a traditional sense of snob or snobbish. It is ironic that it also applies to the sociologists asking the questions, who, as was pointed out (p. 61), also think of themselves as different from and in some senses better than the subjects they are employed to study!

The same resentment against those who identify and collude with the status quo was more brutally expressed in the climactic confrontation of James Kelman's novel *A Disaffection*. The narrative takes place inside the head of Doyle, a Glasgow schoolteacher disillusioned by his role in society, whose unemployed brother accuses him of being a 'middle-class wanker', on which the hero reflects he meant that:

> He was an article that was corrupt. He was representative of corruption, representative of a corrupt and repressive society which operated nicely and efficiently as an effect of the liberal machinations of such as himself, corruptio optimi pessima, not that he was approaching the best but was just a person who had certain tools of the higher-educational processes at his command yet persisted in representing a social order that was not good and was not beneficent to those who have nothing. What right did he have to be treated differently to any member of the fucking government or polis or the fucking law courts in general who sentence you to prison. Doyle had sold his rights.
>
> (Kelman, 1989, p. 303)

WORKING FOR YOURSELF IN THE ENTERPRISE STATE

The foregoing section does not imply that the ruling class, defined in capitalist society by its predominant position in the characteristic institution of a free labour market, is a unitary block, nor that individual employers cannot act against the interests of the ruling class to which they belong and against the system from which they derive their wealth. On the last point, detractors of Marxism often make much of the fact that Marx's analysis of capitalism, as well as his actions intended to hasten its demise, which that analysis predicted, were subsidized by the profits of the Engels's family firm. This was certainly unusual, but the divisions within what Marx called 'the top ten thousand' have already been indicated (p. 29). Indeed, such divisions are complicated by the fact that, in free market – as opposed to state – capitalism, employers, even the largest private monopolies, are incessantly competing with one another, despite cartels and other temporary arrangements between them to corner markets and fix prices. In recent years the splits between sections of the monopoly capitalist ruling class supporting European and American interests have been exacerbated by Britain's increasingly precarious economic position. Corresponding to economic decline, penetration of the economy by American, European and Japanese capital has also increased. The old division between manufacturing and the City has re-emerged with a vengeance following the deregulation of financial markets and the devastation of previously protected productive industry in the name of the freedom of market forces. In addition, employers are, as ever, divided between the few large private monopolies that dominate industry and services alike and the smaller firms that together make up the vast majority of employers, as well as between state and private monopoly capitals.

Small employers in particular exert little influence upon the levers of power in the state. Despite ritual obeisances to their needs by all the parliamentary parties, they are the first to go to the wall in recurrent recessions. Yet they hold an ideological importance far beyond their economic significance. This is not only because of the relative growth of small business in the recent restructuring of capital, so that subcontracting is now more convenient in some areas where new technology has made it feasible for the first time. It is also because the self-employed man (or more occasionally woman) is presented as an ideal for the rest of the employed population to follow. The exceptions that prove the rule – Lady Porter's father, the barrow-boy risen to command a commercial empire – are elevated, not least by themselves, to mythic status. Following Hollywood, the dream is proven as the reality of equality of opportunity, and if the rest of us fail to achieve it then we evidently have only ourselves to blame. More modestly, the ideal of 'working for yourself', of not being employed by anyone and so not having to take orders but being independent, and at the same time not employing others, owing nothing to anyone else and being free of responsibility, is an alluring ideal for very many people. It promises escape from the two main employing and employed classes of the capitalist system. For many working people the ideological appeal of owning your own business promises an end to the exploitation of working for someone else – just as owning your own home is preferred by many to paying rent to a landlord.

This old goal has been revived in a new guise in recent years as individual enterprise has been encouraged by government, both directly, through the enterprise allowance scheme, as an alternative to mass unemployment (see Coffield and MacDonald, 1991) and indirectly through economic restructuring. As a consequence, the numbers of self-employed rose from 442,000 in 1971 to 2.6 million in 1984 (11.2 per cent of the total workforce) and by a further 25 per cent to over 3 million by 1986. By 1990 there were 3,222,000: 2,449,000 men and 773,000 women; 65 per cent of this total had no employees and 33 per cent had fewer than 25 employees (Department of Employment 'Skills and Enterprise Briefing', 13/91). The 'Briefing' noted a negative relationship between self-employment and the trade cycle, resulting in an increase in self-employment during an economic downturn and a decrease during an upturn.

Despite the high failure rate for small business start-ups, self-employment seems a real possibility in many cases because many working people are already able, if not compelled, to supplement their wages or salaries by working for themselves, doing 'jobs on the side' while being employed for regular wages or while unemployed on state benefits. The informal or 'black' economy is enormous and still growing. By definition, estimates of its size can only be approximate. It runs the gamut from youths at traffic lights who wash or mess up car windscreens and the 'models' or 'masseurs' whose adverts plaster telephone booths, to jobbing tradesmen of all sorts. More respectably, teachers give private tuition at night, academics undertake consultancies and surgeons employed by the National Health Service earn their main income from private patients. Indeed, with the growing insecurity inflicted upon more and more employees by the contract culture now permeating what is left of central and local public services, as well as with the corporate restructurings along the same lines of many of the largest private companies, such 'moonlighting' is becoming essential to many people's basic survival.

The purpose of 'moonlighting' has been defined by Polsky (1971, p. 91) as 'not merely to provide more income but to provide it in a way that allows you to keep your primary job'. Hobbs (1990), who quoted this definition, showed its continuity not only with the well-known phenomenon of white-collar crime, which runs from pilfering office stationery to billion-dollar computer crime, and from the abuse of perks, such as making personal calls on office phones, to fiddling discounts and expenses. He also showed how it fits into a traditional pattern of working-class entrepreneurship or 'fiddling' – goods falling off the back of lorries or out of warehouses and the general black market in 'hot' or stolen items – which he saw as peculiar to the old East End of London but which is more or less developed everywhere. Indeed, it possibly originates in the paradox, which socialists used often to point at, of workers making goods they do not own. Today, in times of economic crisis, as Hobbs (1990) said, such 'Entrepreneurship is an increasingly attractive option' (p. 196). The 'business' of Hobbs's title merges 'legal and illegal methodology into one neutralizing or justificatory term'. Thus the universal claim that ' "I'm a business man" provides a touchstone for those aspiring to entrepreneurship' and links the legal to the illegal entrepreneur (p. 166). It also typically includes the self-employed businessman, where self-employment shades into the informal economy of the so-called 'underclass'. The stereotype is represented in television's Arthur Daley, whose pretensions to the respectability of 'Daley's Into Europe plc' are shared by 'Trotters' Independent Traders of New York, Paris and Peckham' in another 1980s TV series.

Hobbs's East End 'jump-up', like the Liverpudlian 'scally', 'negotiates a living by partaking in any activity that proffers pecuniary reward without engaging him in the normative contractual arrangement suggested by employer–employee relationships' (p. 155). To the extent that they are successful in living from the proceeds of their 'business' – and Hobbs's cast of colourful characters extends within one pub from clients to small businessmen and the local criminal elite – the jump-ups, scallies or conventional criminals really do constitute a true underclass outside the labour market and not ideologically fabricated out of the unemployed. However, there is a countertendency that has been repeatedly noted for successful criminals, from the Krays to the US mafia – the latter vividly shown in Scorsese's film *Goodfellas* – to move back into the labour market as employers buying into 'legit' or respectable businesses. All such 'business' is, however, as Hobbs pointed out, essentially parasitic. It typically involves acting as middlemen in the circulation, not the production, of commodities. In the new mixed public/private economy of state-subsidized private enterprise, as well as in the privatized sections of the franchise state, 'all aspects of life including major institutions and professions . . . are subject to negotiation' (Hobbs, 1990, p. 181). 'Flexibility' and 'adaptability' are the keywords of the new enterprise state, in which increasingly anything goes but which has been encouraged by successive Conservative governments that themselves considerably widened the scope of legitimate public governance (see 'Thatcher, the sleaze factor', *Private Eye*, 23 November 1990, for just a thin scraping from the tip of a very large and dirty iceberg).

Encouraged by the predominant message of mass media advertising that it is possible to get something for nothing, or at least to get a lot for very little, the new self-employed have much expanded the petit bourgeoisie recognized by classical class analysis. Historically this was made up of small shopkeepers, farmers, traders, contractors and all those self-employed who owned their own means of production but did not invest capital in the employment of others. It was a class in – if not for – itself, especially in countries where small farming was the predominant form of agriculture. An apparently insignificant and relatively powerless stratum of society, the classical petit bourgeoisie was invested at different times with almost diabolic potential. This was because in the Marxist view, which derives individual consciousness from position in society, the petit bourgeoisie shared aspects of proletarian class consciousness, from its position *vis-à-vis* the capitalist ruling class, combined with a bourgeois outlook typified by thinking itself superior to and different from the working class. The petit bourgeoisie was therefore characteristically Janus-faced, vacillating and untrustworthy. 'Petit bourgeois deviations' were recurrently rooted out of the international communist movement, for fully developed they could lead the workers back on to the capitalist path. The petit bourgeoisie allied to the lumpenproletariat was regarded as a particularly virulent combination and indeed was the social basis for fascism according, for instance, to Trotsky (himself denounced as a petit bourgeois by his rival Stalin).

From a socialist and cooperative point of view, the leaders of the old communist parties were indeed right to distrust these individuals who owed no allegiance to anyone but themselves. Despite the fact that most of the self-employed today are merely ordinary working people trying to make a go of things for themselves, whose ventures normally fail in times of crisis faced by the consolidation of existing monopolies, the higher up you go and the nearer to the ownership of capital, the more savings and resources that you have, the easier it is for you to employ your own capital in your own interest. Eventually, if you are successful, you do nothing else but employ other people to work for you (or for someone else, if you invest and speculate elsewhere) and thus join the employing and financial class. The same applies the more skilled and qualified that you are: the easier it is to work for yourself by selling your specialized services, instead of being employed by someone to perform them; for example, top freelance journalists, computer systems analysts, financial consultants, etc. If you live like this for long enough, you start to see yourself as not belonging to either the employed or the employing classes, and may then adopt the illusory assumption that you are outside the system altogether. The influence of such illusions is not limited to the relatively small numbers of the self-employed, however, but can affect the employed as well, so that people who do nothing else but sell their labour to live can imagine they are free spirits because they own their own house, possess a few shares, do what they like in their free time and so on. Perhaps the illusion that they make their millions by their own efforts and not by employing other people to work for them also appeals to even the largest employers and financial speculators.

Certainly the ideal of the individual entrepreneur is central to the ideology of enterprise, which, as Frank Coffield (1990) said, 'perhaps more than any other term summarises the *zeitgeist* created by the Conservative government during the 1980s'. However, he warned, 'We are not dealing with a tightly defined, agreed and unitary concept but with a farrago of "hurrah" words like "creativity", "initiative" and "leadership".' In the name of enterprise, 'employers have been given by Government increasing responsibilities to run hospitals, polytechnics, universities and schools. And yet the economic performance of British industry, as judged by the highest trade deficit in our history in 1989, is a dismal record of failure in international competition.' This showed, he argued, 'the triumph of political preference over experience'. Yet it is perhaps more than this and, as has been suggested (p. 23), 'the enterprise solution' has been advanced as a form of modernization and a way out of the intractable crisis of Keynesian welfare capitalism.

'State induced enterprise', as Wallace and Chandler (1989) called it, is coming to 'permeate the franchise sections of the welfare state' from youth training managing agents, to schools, colleges, the health and social services, along with whatever other public services can be put out to contract. As an organizational principle it means that 'problems can be privatised too' and 'whilst responsibility is de-centralised, power is further centralised'. This mirrors 'the model of the state as a holding company which sub-contracts parts of itself at different levels'. This gives, as Randall (1992, p. 4) wrote, 'the sort of freedom which business people gain through franchising with a Pizza Hut multinational'. Or, as Ainley and Corney (1990, p. 136) put it, 'A clear advantage' of what they called 'government by quango' is that 'the government can retain firm control of policy development but distance itself from the detailed day-to-day management of programmes. Additionally, Civil Service bureaucracies can be expanded and disbanded "to task", according to the exigencies that arise . . . This new flexibility of response allowed [Conservative] government to by-pass and eradicate the remnants of Britain's corporatist and tri-partite past.' In the private sector too, 'The processes of managerial decentralisation are associated with an "entrepreneurial" rather than a "bureaucratic" model of management and a correspondingly greater emphasis upon initiative, flexibility and autonomy as opposed to legal/rational routine' (Hickox and Moore, 1992, p. 108).

In this new 'mixed economy' of private and state capital, not only have former services provided by the local or national state been taken over and sold off to private companies, as have, for instance, many local bus services, or the national power and water industries. Other public services are retained by the state as semi-independent agencies to be run at a profit, as the Conservatives plan for the health service. Former state monopolies that sold services at a profit, such as telecommunications, have also been broken up and made to compete for their customers. Consumers are then redefined as 'citizens' with individual 'rights' enshrined in the contractual relations of 'charters'. Aside from the fact that British subjects of the Crown are not 'citizens' in any of the senses that the term acquired through the French revolution, which originally popularized it – let alone the abuse of the word 'charter', associated as it once was with Chartism – this is a spurious individualism that owes much to what would classically have been called 'petit bourgeois ideology'. The 'citizens' of Mr Major's 'charters' do not participate collectively as informed citizens in the democratic decisions about which goods and services should be provided by society at what cost to its members. They merely choose as passive consumers between the different commodities that the market offers them. Their 'equality' is only that of the marketplace, in which, as has often been said, all are free to dine at the Ritz, but most of us cannot afford it.

The only common value of commodities is their relative price. Commodity consciousness cannot therefore accept real, qualitative differences but must always compare the goods and services on offer as either better or worse, measured as more or less in terms of monetary values. Like the illusion (referred to on p. 10) that the expression of complex problems in mathematical form necessarily renders them more scientific and amenable to logical control, the apparent objectivity of monetary measures actually masks the subjective value judgements that are being made. This is because, as the Roman Emperor Vespasian retorted to the ministers who objected to his tax upon lavatories, 'money does not smell'. As the tool of all tools in which all qualities are represented as quantities, money appears as a universal medium, a measure which is not itself measured, standing quite apart from all the various commodities for which it can be exchanged (see Simmel, 1978). This is most plainly shown in the weird distortions of the grossly inflated art market, itself a consequence of the lack of outlet for productive investment, where one painting or artist cannot be accepted as different from another, but must be ranked along a scale of millions of pounds. All sense of real artistic skill and the complementary and contrasted qualities of different artistic visions is thus lost.

Ethical values also disappear in money prices; as the founder of the Amstrad computer company and 1980s icon of enterprise, Alan Sugar, said, if he could have made as much profit from selling miniaturized atomic weapons as from computers then he would have done so. Similarly, imponderable and uncertain qualities, such as education – the future of which is ever in doubt, because who knows how the ideas of the past will be reinterpreted by future generations? – are reduced to simple certainties that can easily be measured: spelling and elementary maths, for example. Public issues of health and welfare are likewise disguised by the mechanical routines of cost accounting. And, once established, monetary measures of 'value added' form a closed, apparently concrete and completely self-sufficient system of reference exclusive of all external considerations. The end result is a new Benthamism in which profit is the only measure of utility, so that, as was said of a previous indictment of such 'hard times', 'As the issues are reduced to algebraic formulation they are patently emptied of all real meaning' (Leavis, 1972, p. 265).

The money economy thus intrudes ever more insistently to degrade and devalue even intimate human relations to monetary terms. The individual pays for everything and our freedom from what money can buy is ever more limited. Thus individualism is heightened again and it becomes harder to see things from a wider social or even global perspective, let alone to have any influence upon events. This is a paradox at a time when it is also becoming increasingly obvious to growing numbers of people that the present closed economic cycle of producing more and more commodities for sale in order to realize the profits to produce more and more commodities cannot continue for much longer without inflicting irreparable damage upon the environment that sustains human life. Thus wider implications impinge ever more insistently at the same time that commodification of services for sale removes whole areas of human existence from consideration in terms of the larger social and ecological systems of which they form a part. Instead, they are lost in an apparent economic objectivity beyond any judgement of their real worth. Education, which, as has been noted, is vital to the transmission of values to the future generations but which is by its nature inherently uncertain, has been degraded more than most public services in the new enterprise state. In our schools and colleges the commodification of uncertain qualities is reducing the aims of education to narrowly specified and supposedly objective outcomes that can easily be measured and compared. This process is not unconnected, it will be argued, with the growing importance of education in sustaining new forms of class division as the old ones have broken down.

EDUCATION AND THE MIDDLE CLASS

Once they overcame their initial hostility to publicly provided education, Britain's rulers began belatedly in the nineteenth century to provide through the state basic schooling for the majority of the population. The patrician and paternalistic attitude remained that state education for the masses was an elementary and second-best preparation for labouring life. It provided only the basic literacy and numeracy that most work and social life was coming to require, together with additional technical skills acquired through apprenticeship. The grammar schools and redbrick universities were also seen as vocationally serving the growing middle class by preparing them for non-manual, professional occupations. In this rigidly stratified tripartite world the elite private schools were seen as separate from and superior to the state schools, grammar and elementary/secondary modern. This was still the attitude of recent Conservative governments, none of whose ministers sent their own children to the state schools – certainly not state secondaries, even the opted-out ones – for which they were responsible. However, ironically it was the Conservatives who first blurred the distinction between state and private education with their 1979 scheme of assisted places to private schools. This reinvented a hybrid direct-grant system and so subsidized the private sector with scholarships paid for out of the public purse. The 1988 Education Reform Act subsequently attempted to cut all schools (and, later, polytechnics and other higher and further education as well as tertiary and sixth-form colleges) free of local authority control to compete for pupils in the marketplace.

While it was ostensibly aimed at restoring the grammar school 'excellence' yearned for, it was suggested, by a new breed of grammar-school-educated Tories, the logic of this marketing of education led towards a state-subsidized privatization that would eventually put all schools on the same financial footing as the private schools, though without their inherited privileged position at the top of the market. The process of marketization paralleled what has been called the market modernization of the new enterprise state. Following the precedent set by the Department of Employment's previous funding of youth training, in such a system of semi-private agencies each school or college would receive central government grants according to the number of pupils or students it attracted. The independent schools could have no objections to joining such a state system, in which they would still be able to select pupils and charge fees. In return they would receive government grants for every pupil they already had. Instead of the state taking over the private sector, as Labour had always advocated if not implemented, the intention was to subsidize the privatization of the public sector. The division between private and public would then be lost in the competition between state-subsidized independent institutions. This was Mrs Thatcher's vision of what one of her education ministers called a 'new partnership between parents and the state'.

The eventual outcome of this independent budgeting would be to strengthen the position of already 'successful' schools and colleges, while the market forces of parental choice would close the 'least successful'. At the same time, schools could begin to charge fees for more facilities or 'extras' (as the 1987 Education Act put it), just as colleges would provide courses at full cost to students who could take out loans to pay if they did not already have the money from their parents. As in the private schools sector, 'extras' might soon include better equipment, smaller classes and more qualified teachers attracted by higher salaries, while in the colleges only the better-off students would be able to afford the more expensive courses at prestigious departments in the most renowned colleges (predictably at the antique universities).

The testing of children at seven, eleven, fourteen and sixteen was intended to provide an indication to parents of the 'success' or otherwise of competing schools. For that reason test results had to be simplified down to raw scores in a few basic spelling and maths exercises. The importance of such arbitrary educational selection is heightened by the growing insecurity that has been noted, even for the top 20 per cent of school-leavers previously guaranteed access to careers in supervisory or administrative, non-manual employment by good school performance. Now that degree-level higher education is required for entry to more and more professional and managerial occupations, there is greater dependence upon academic achievement as the means of reproducing superior status, with greater resort by those who can afford it to private schooling. Further, it has been suggested that culturally arbitrary educational credentials assume a new importance in sustaining cultural distinctions in the absence of clear-cut divisions between the formerly manually working class and the traditionally non-manual middle class. For those who think of themselves and would like to think of their children as middle rather than working class, educational credentials have a new significance. This parental demand contributes to the widening differentiation between state schools that the Education Reform Act was designed to encourage. Meanwhile, in this academic competition, the attempt to construct a vocationally relevant education for the rest of the school population has been abandoned.

The overall effect of marketing education is to strengthen the traditional British system of educational selection, in which failure is the norm. For the majority, education is an effort in which at each hurdle only a minority continue to the next stage. The testing of children from the age of seven will begin this process even earlier. It previously started at eleven-plus, when a minority were selected for grammar schooling. In comprehensive schools the age of selection was then raised progressively to fourteen, where the few sheep who would attempt O level were segregated from the remainder of goats bound to take the second-rate CSE examinations. With the introduction of GCSE the age of selection was further raised to sixteen, when, again, only a minority pass at the A to C levels required for the next stage. It has only recently become the case that a majority of children do not leave at this age; a majority of boys still do so. This can be compared with what happens in the USA and Canada, where there is national concern for the 20 per cent of 'high school drop-outs' who leave before they are eighteen. Among the 20 per cent or so remaining to eighteen in England and Wales a third of those attempting the A level entrance exams for higher education fall at the fence, and for the rest the grades they obtain determine their level of entry to an elaborate hierarchy of colleges and universities. Only those graduates attaining the highest-class marks are deemed worthy of pursuing further study, while at postgraduate level the majority of candidates fail to complete their doctoral theses. The contest is heightened by increased competition between colleges, with new selective distinctions being introduced for qualifications (between 'good firsts' and 'lower firsts', for instance) to replace those discredited by larger numbers passing them 'lower down' the system. In this way the educational system in Britain performs what Durkheim (1979) suggested was the prime function of a university, in the sense of an organized body of professional teachers providing for its own perpetuation.

In the new mixed economy of state-subsidized privatized contract and competition, this is not the only object of the education system, though it may be the only one perceived by most of those teaching in the universities. The hope of those who advocate the application of a free market to education is that the league tables of schools and colleges that will result will hide the realities of the previously sharp divisions that caused such resentment at eleven-plus and, later, at fourteen between O levels and CSEs. This intention is of course contradicted by the enthusiasts for grammar schooling, whose whole aim is to reintroduce the old distinctions, with all their traditional rigour. These traditionalists also oppose any watering-down of the A level gold standard for entry to higher education in favour of a mass system of education and training, such as some educational free-marketeers support. Traditionalists seek to reintroduce O levels for some in place of GCSEs for all, and oppose the ending of the binary division between the universities and other higher education institutions. Yet, rather than retaining academic distinctions between universities and polytechnics, the free market, it is argued by its supporters, will heighten distinctions of quality between and within institutions of higher education but along a widening scale. Predictably this polarization will be accentuated by the separation of teaching from research, leaving a reborn polytechnic and college sector as teaching-only colleges at the bottom of the league.

As with the league tables of schools based upon their test results, it is intended that the heightened polarities will correspond to and will reproduce the new 'classlessness'. This has supposedly dissolved the traditional tripartite divisions into a mass of individuals competing from starting positions that are assumed to have been equalized. The associated cultures of achievement and apprenticeship of the old tripartism have also been obviated by the new means of access to acquiring knowledge and skills made explicit by the information now provided by new technology and aided by new systems of vocational qualifications, flexibility and credit accumulation and transfer. These new sources of knowledge and its certification also remove the monopoly upon education of schools and colleges, so that qualifications can as easily be acquired at work or in the community, creating in the vision of some enthusiasts 'a learning society' driven by the market for new vocational skills.

Enthusiasts for the new correspondence of market education with a 'classless' and meritocratic society do not recognize that individuals in the new middle-working class are already ranked in a hierarchy according to their parents' cultural capital and to their material status, which more or less corresponds to it, fluid though this correspondence maybe in an economic situation of endemic crises and rapid sectoral transformations. Only at the base and top of the scale is it recognized that traditional cultures close access to the new system of education. In the least successful, 'dependent' and 'problem' council schools, members of the stigmatized 'underclass' are seen as trapped by a culture of poverty and low aspiration. The fear of relegation to this uncertificated underclass would, it was intended, act as a spur to achievement within the system of testing and examination, in the same way as the carrots of scholarships and selective entry to 'successful' schools along the differentiated scale of opted-out, technical and magnet schools that the marketeers hope the 1988 Act will encourage. At the top of the tree, private education, increasingly subsidized not only by parental donations and fees but also by state allowances and charitable exemptions, if not yet directly by vouchers or credits, is protected by the sanctity of 'freedom of choice' that it represents and to which, it is claimed, the whole education system is increasingly open.

Only to the elite upper stratum that can afford to have its offspring educated privately and intensively from an early age, through a succession of nurses, nannies, preparatory and boarding schools to an extended childhood at sheltered colleges, finishing schools and military academies, does achievement in this system remain effortless. Although, as Simmel and later Bourdieu noted, for those who do succeed in the uphill struggle, 'the accumulation of intellectual achievements . . . gives a rapidly growing and disproportionate advantage to those who are favoured by it [so that] the highest stages of education require less effort for every step further than the lower stages, and yet at the same time produce greater results' (Simmel, 1978, p. 442). Thus for Simmel no less than for Bourdieu,

> The apparent equality with which educational materials are available to everyone interested in them is, in reality, a sheer mockery. The same is true of the other freedoms accorded by liberal doctrines which, though they certainly do not hamper the individual from gaining goods of whatever kind, do however disregard the fact that only those already privileged in some way or another have the possibility of acquiring them. For just as the substance of education – in spite of, or because of its general availability – can ultimately be acquired only through individual activity, so it gives rise to the most intangible and thus the most unassailable aristocracy, to a distinction between high and low which can be abolished neither (as can socioeconomic differences) by a decree or revolution, nor by the will of those concerned. Thus it was appropriate for Jesus to say to the rich youth: 'Give away your goods to the poor', but not for him to say 'Give your education to the underprivileged'.
> (Simmel, 1978, pp. 339–40)

The result is, as Simmel added, that 'There is no advantage that appears to those in inferior positions to be so despised, and before which they feel so deprived and helpless, as the advantage of education' (p. 340). This is the deepest wound among many of what Sennet and Cobb (1973) called the 'hidden injuries of class' that are inflicted upon the majority of the population by the present social system. From this come the terrible admissions, which can be heard so often from ordinary people and even from their children at a very early age ('I'm not brainy', 'I'm thick'), and many people's readiness, not only through exhaustion or because of lack of resources, to settle for what they acknowledge is too often trashy and second-rate. So too comes the secret contempt for theory and culture, indeed for generalized thinking that goes far beyond the commonly accepted and easily understood, which is another of the crippling debilities of the English cultural inheritance. It is questionable whether this cultural complex can be unravelled by the material incentives provided to individuals to compete for access to the 'better' schools and colleges, for qualifications guaranteeing entry to more secure and more rewarding occupations and preventing their relegation to semi-employment and state dependency. It is more likely that academic competition will reinforce the unequal positions from which it starts. It is also doubtful that the majority will for long accept their necessary relative 'failure' within a system that confirms the elevation of the few and affirms against supposedly objective, academic criteria the stupidity of the masses – especially as the consequences of the incrementally rapid pace of historical change worldwide impinge ever more insistently upon even the most obdurate and self-isolated individuals.

CLASS CONSCIOUSNESS IN A NEW WORLD ORDER

Little Englandism, the narrowness and parochialism of the world view upon which the traditional hierarchical structures of English society have been sustained, is often remarked as the source of the peculiarities of the English. This cultural isolation is crumbling, and for Euro-market enthusiasts this represents a liberation, allowing individuals to free themselves from the local and regional affinities of class and custom behind which they have sheltered for so long. At the same time the Conservative governments that opened the door to the single European market retained an abiding ambivalence to the new integration with the world economy that they proposed. This arose not only from their commitment to City financiers, trading upon the remnants of the pound's position as a leading world currency, but also from slavish adherence by successive British governments to the foreign policy priorities of the United States of America. These counter-pressures to full European integration have fuelled a reaction to what is presented by the populist press as foreign interference in Britain's sovereign affairs. External threats to the supposedly unitary 'national way of life' range from petty bureaucratic incursions by the 'Belgian Empire' to more sinister 'waves' of immigrants supposedly queuing on the other side of the Chunnel and have already punctured the national psyche of the sceptred isle set in its silver sea. The ultimate threat conjured up here is not the despised 'Frogs', as the French are still regularly referred to by *The Sun* newspaper, nor the indignity of rule by the 'Krauts' (ditto), twice defeated in two world wars, nor even the Portuguese, Slavs and southern Italians on the fringes of the market, but beyond them the Turks, Arabs, black and Asian poor of the Third World. Against this external threat class divisions can anneal into a common white Britishness, directed in the first instance at the inner-city internal colonies of black settlement.

The assertion by 'the Brits' – the invention seems again to be *The Sun*'s – of a common Britishness (though brutishness, as the great Scots poet Hugh MacDiarmid said, would be more appropriate) also has the virtue of burying the claims to nationhood on equal status with the other European countries of Scotland and Wales and of Irish unification within the EC. However, it contradicts the widening appreciation by more and more people that the gathering economic and ecological crises pose problems for the future of humanity that cannot be solved within the confines of any single nation state but require international solutions.

In the era of the single European market and what ex-Premier Heath called 'the new imperialism' of a single superpower (BBC1, 7 February 1991), a new world order is called for from all sides. There are two versions of this vision, however: one is presented by the President of the US superpower, which politically now dominates the UN and whose military might was demonstrated in its desolation of Iraq, a former Third World client state built up to relative prosperity for its war against Iran; the other is an inchoate and uncoordinated demand from the majority of the world's people for economic justice, and increasingly for the very possibility of human survival. This cry for a future is amplified within the metropolitan countries by all those who place themselves on the side of the downtrodden and oppressed. It is echoed by those who see that the new world order proposed by the US President can only succeed in accelerating the destruction of the environment and deepening the impoverishment of the majority to provide the cheap raw materials and super-exploited labour upon which a metropolitan minority depends to sustain its overdevelopment. This is the same imperialism that has shaped the terrible contours of the twentieth century, from the build-up to two wars for redivision of the world with which it opened, to the world crisis with which it is closing.

The forces of the left that once opposed imperialism no longer recognize in it the chief obstacle to further human progress. In Britain this is because the legacy of empire preserved traditional class relations in the post-1945 social democratic compromise that only broke down irretrievably at the end of the long boom after 1973. In addition, the left in Britain as elsewhere was confused and then divided by the transformation of the first socialist state into an imperial superpower – a transformation in the Soviet Union signalled definitively by its invasion of Czechoslovakia in 1968. Now the Russian empire has disintegrated as the consequence of losing the Cold War for world hegemony with the United States (a competition it appeared to be winning for a time, from the US defeat in Vietnam to its own defeat in Afghanistan), those on the left who retained their faith in Soviet communism are utterly demoralized. Even the alternative to the deformation of socialism into national socialism that was presented by the Chinese cultural revolution has ended in, perhaps temporary, defeat. National liberation movements therefore no longer model themselves upon either of the two alternatives that Russia and then China for a time held up to capitalist development. Indeed, oppressed nationalities are more likely to pose their demands, if not in religious terms, then in the same language of equality, freedom and democracy with which the West justifies the deepening inequities of its new world order.

The slogans of nineteenth-century revolution cannot today be realized without the destruction of the imperial system that resulted from the development of the capitalism that those revolutions in a handful of Western countries unleashed. To a Third World observer the alternatives are clear: 'the objective necessity for a reform of the world system; failing this, the only way out is through the worst barbarity, the genocide of entire peoples' (Amin, 1989, p. 114). From such a viewpoint, in any country 'social classes are not defined exclusively by their position in the local system but – and no less significantly – by their relationship to the range of forces operating on a world scale' (Amin, 1989, p. 5).

The social polarization that has been described as taking place in Britain under the label of Thatcherism has resulted in the paradox that, with the erosion of traditional class divisions, especially the conventional manual/mental divide between the classical working and middle classes, material inequalities have increased but the perception of them has become blurred so that there is thus an apparent homogenization of the new working middle of metropolitan society. Even as the scale along which status differences based upon wealth are measured is stretched, increased insecurity and the volatility of individual careers meld the perceptions of the majority towards a new classlessness; or, rather, the tendency is towards a new middle-working-classness marked by the boundaries between the employing and ruling class above and the new rough 'underclass' beneath. This is a fluid situation, however, in which what Zuboff (1988) called 'the sedimented beliefs' left by previous periods still play a part and in which 'the magnetism of the past and the forces of inertia on which it thrives' as well as 'contemporary events' can 'reanimate meanings normally associated with an earlier historical epoch' (p. 233). Yet how far the new 'respectable' and 'responsible' public opinion in the working middle of society can be united with their rulers above against external enemies and their internal representatives was shown not only by the war against Argentina that secured Mrs Thatcher's second term but also by the more complete unanimity that supported Britain's participation in the US-led barbarity against Iraq.

The classical proletarian identification with an international working class has been lost in the West, along with the social conditions that originally gave rise to that ideology. Instead, it is perhaps true to say, as Laborit (1977, p. 150) did, that 'a person "feels" bourgeois or proletarian according as he or she "feels" sufficiently gratified or not by the hierarchical system' of commodity production, so that nowadays 'the bourgeoisie and the proletariat are distinguished much more by subjective experience than by socio-economic criteria'. However, to say that you are as oppressed and as working class as you feel does not seem a very secure basis upon which to build anew the opposition to imperialism for an alternative world order. Perhaps the search for unity beyond the fragments, for which progressive forces in the West have long been seeking, can no longer necessarily be expressed in terms of class. Perhaps the terms of unity are better expressed by different sections of the population, who together make up the majority recognizing in different ways and at different times that it is no longer possible to continue in the destructive closed cycle of commodity production but that for the sake of a common future some way of breaking out to the larger global environment must be found before that ecology irretrievably breaks down.

Such a collective assertion must go beyond the demand for a cultural pluralism that is too easily accommodated to the discrete markets that capitalism continuously creates and re-creates. In terms of nationality too, it is not enough to oppose cultural uniformity in the name of multicultural variety, for this can also be degraded to the separate and supposedly equal development of a new apartheid. It is the ideological and material construction of a more or less racially defined 'underclass' that must chiefly be opposed by those who seek to build upon an identification with the mass of exploited humanity against the degradation of its indigenous cultures and the common environment we all share. Racism cannot be allowed to become respectable for those who assert that there are no subhuman beings. Beyond pluralism and multiculturalism a new basis for unity must be defined to take the place of the old proletarian internationalism. That new basis for a common humanity is being created in the many struggles by various sections of the population against the particular evils that individually oppress them. They can find their common denominator in the demand for an end to imperialism and the danger that its relentless expansion and competition poses to the future of humanity.

This is not to advocate a return to the old 'anti-imperialist alliances' with which the new left of the 1960s sought to revive its flagging campaigns, and still less to urge the necessity for a vanguard party to unify and direct the various campaigns. In fact, with the dissolution of the classical factory proletariat in the West, no one organization can any longer aspire to unite the old manual working class with the mental abilities but economic powerlessness of the old intellectuals – or at least the 'progressive' ones who were prepared to join the old communist parties. Instead, it is the role of a new intelligentsia to inform the various and disparate social struggles with a wider global political perspective that takes them beyond immediate demands that can inevitably only be met in part and at the expense of other oppressed and working people and our common environment. Relentless critical analysis (what Mrs Thatcher used to call 'perpetual moaning') is needed to draw the connections between and organize the support for the various opposition movements the present system inevitably generates in many different sections of the population. More and more people, beyond the old intelligentsia of specialized information workers – teachers, writers, scientists, even sociologists – are able to make these connections as new technology informates society. Sociology in particular is well placed to raise general questions of social finality and individual purpose; as long, that is, as sociologists can free themselves from the constraints upon them of policy-directed research and if they can manage to communicate not just for their own benefit to other sociologists but also to a wider public.

In terms of skills, the rapid diffusion of new technology throughout society, while it obviates previously specialized crafts, also provides the catalyst for the majority of people to begin to think again in a generalized way about social questions. For not only are the latest applications of new technology part of the unprecedented acceleration of social change, which of itself stimulates thought and loosens the hold upon a changing reality of old mental paradigms, but new technology also presents information in new forms and demolishes the old divisions between previously discrete bodies of information. However, for information to be transformed by the unique human capacity to envisage alternative futures into the knowledge that action is necessary now to avert destruction in the near future requires a combination of widened access to information technology with the democratic forms necessary to act upon the information acquired. Only information combined with democracy can provide the skills necessary for survival.

In class terms the common goal of struggle by the majority for a sustainable future can be posed against the uncertain gains privileged individuals can hope for from safeguarding their positions of relative advantage in the existing hierarchy. And as the situation worsens there is growing realization that international efforts are required to meet the emergencies of ecological degradation and associated climatic change. The only (British) historical precedent for the challenge presented to survival by the ecological consequences of the continuing uninhibited expansion of capital through the latest imperial world order is that faced by society in the last national emergency during the Second World War. This time, however, no society can hope to meet the challenge alone, while within society alliance on terms of equality with cooperation and planning will be required, now as then, merely to survive.

Meanwhile, it is the struggle for daily individual survival that continues to preoccupy the mass of the population. In this effort to preserve some security in an increasingly insecure social and economic situation, education, it has been argued, has come to assume a renewed importance. This is not only because education promises a better future than government can deliver in the present through an economy over which it exercises diminishing control. It is also because the alternative futures to which education can lead represent alternative ways of using new technology. Old cultural distinctions rendered increasingly arbitrary by their lack of correspondence with rapidly changing material circumstances can be preserved by the selection of a minority through an antique and academic curriculum. In this case the facility of new technology for reducing cultural qualities to arbitrary quantities can be used to produce elaborate and supposedly objective rank orderings of individuals in a reanimated hierarchy. Then, as Laborit (1977, p. 153) observed, 'the more the hierarchical system is staggered and individualised, the greater the sovereignty of the commodity'. Alternatively, new technology can be used to its best effect in production by charging social and economic processes with information that is accessible to the collective contributions of all involved. Its tendency is to share information and raise skills generally, multiskilling the majority, empowering their democratic participation to control their personal choice of the commodities presented to them, and generalizing power to control the future direction of society and its relations to the world economy and ecology of which it is a part. Beyond individual freedom, with all its limitations, free societies might then find new collective purpose in giving themselves over to securing the survival of the species.

Chapter 6

Conclusion – Skills for Survival

A model [has been] described. This model is a simplification and an idealisation and consequently a falsification. It is hoped that the features retained for discussion are those of the greatest importance in the present state of knowledge.
 (Alan Turing, on the chemical basis of morphogenesis. Quoted in Hodges, 1983, p. 363)

The latest applications of new technology are producing a situation that is widely recognized. It was succinctly expressed by Henri Laborit, whose cybernetic vision has informed much of this book's perspective on the changing divisions of labour and knowledge:

> Since modern societies consume more and more specialised information, and less and less mechanical labour power, the law of supply and demand results in the establishment of economic hierarchies of occupational power which are based more on specialised information than on mechanical labour (which carries only a small information content). The length of time spent on schooling increases; and there is occupational retraining, that is to say, occupational life is recharged with information.
> (Laborit, 1977, p. 117)

However, Laborit distinguished between 'occupational information, which introduces the individual into the process of commodity production, and generalised information, [which] concerns structures rather than facts. It concerns the general laws which enable people to organise facts' (pp. 11-12). 'What is important' for generalized knowledge 'is the social structure, the whole set of relations between the elements in the social set' (p. 122). For information, as Laborit agreed, is power and the desirable objective is to generalize power. 'Generalised power is only possible if there is also generalised information which permits action at every level of organisation' (p. 155). These are not merely moral prescriptions or political preferences: they indicate the direction society must take if its modernization is to contribute to the international cooperation that is necessary to ensure future human survival.

Learning at all levels is vital for the communication of generalized and specialized information through education and training, and the importance of learning for modernization is widely recognized. Education and training policy has been foregrounded in this account because talk about learning is talk about society itself, what values it should preserve in the young and what shape it should take in the future. The goal of education and training policy can no longer be the attempt made by social democracy in the past to equalize the starting points of individuals so that they can compete on equal terms for unequal places in the employment hierarchy. Nor can it be, as it was during education's vocational phase from 1976 to 1987, to fuel the competition between national capitals in a destructive and exploitative race for economic supremacy. Rhetoric about Britain 'catching up with Germany and Japan' by becoming a 'high-productivity, high-skill economy' involves, as a Conservative Employment Secretary once admitted, 'leaving labour-intensive, unskilled work to others' (Norman Fowler, speech to the Bow Group, 23 October 1989). He was referring to the sweated labour of the Third World, but Norman Tebbit when he was Employment Minister advocated driving down domestic wages to Hong Kong levels. The Conservative strategy within Europe also seemed at times to aim at keeping Britain as the poor man of the continent, so as to attract multinational companies seeking a bridgehead into the EC to invest in the country. For education this implied low-level vocational training for the majority and reborn grammar schooling for an academic minority.

Now the 1988 Education Reforms have proclaimed academic competition for all, but this has less to do with any economic modernization than with an attempt to reinstate the old tripartite class world of upper, middle and working class. The reforms have no correspondence with the labour market and posit parents rather than employers as the consumers of education. The claims to open meritocracy made for the new arrangements are shown to be a sham by the increasing inequalities of the starting points in the competition. Such claims are a diversion from the demands for economic modernization made upon new entrants to the workforce, which at any level do not include proficiency in an outdated and academic curriculum.

In fact, with the relative decline of British industry and the growth of multinational companies decreasing the influence that any government can exercise over its national economy, education and training policy has come to assume an unwarranted importance over more fundamental problems facing society. One lesson of the accidental and short-lived boom upon which the economy stumbled in 1986 was that vocational education and regional and equal opportunities programmes all rely for their success on a well-functioning national economy and labour market. They can only complement economic recovery, not substitute for it. This does not imply that educational, training and equal opportunities policies are unnecessary, just that the primary emphasis should always be upon sustaining a balanced economic development.

As a first step the full employment goal of economic policy must be reasserted. The right to work must be affirmed as well as the right to training, which has been substituted for it but is often not training at all, i.e. the right to work with proper training. Training without jobs is rightly perceived as pointless; employers should have a duty to provide training to agreed standards to anyone under eighteen whom they employ and all workers should have the right to paid day-release and sabbaticals for education or training. Access to training for 'good' jobs with 'prospects' must remain open beyond sixteen. This is the single most effective way of ensuring that more young people remain in full-time education and do not leave at the earliest opportunity in the hope of getting one of the few remaining skilled jobs available locally. Staying-on rates for females have already risen beyond 50 per cent, owing to young women remaining in school or going to college to obtain the further qualifications necessary for them to gain access to many office jobs. Youth training, such as it is, only sustains and aggravates the outdated apprentice-boy model of training. This is inappropriate to industry that is no longer so labour-intensive and that has a rapid rate of technological change. If employers cannot actually guarantee employment after training – for the trainee to remain for a period after training, as in the old articles of apprenticeship – training must be to standards that are at least credible in local labour markets. Minimum wages and protective labour legislation for young workers should also be reinstated.

In place of the moribund market modernization attempted by the Conservatives there is the potential for an alliance between what is left of British industrial capital and a government that would attempt a real modernization of industry and society. This opportunity was thrown away with the 1992 general election result. In its context advances could have been made towards a more open, relevant and less hierarchical education and training system. The first priority for any government seriously committed to real modernization would be to re-establish the purpose of education, science and the arts in society: to stimulate thought and develop new knowledge and skills to deal with a rapidly changing reality. As the National Union of Teachers put it in 1990: 'The love of learning, the ability to learn and the confidence to learn must be the central objectives of schools.' It is easy to say that education should be about liberation or empowerment but it is vital to establish this as a goal of policy because it is the contradiction between education's liberatory promise and its repressive selective function that is at the root of so much disenchantment with the education system as it is (especially secondary schooling, where the selective pressures for future employment are still most acute). Participation by as many people as possible is what is required for a democratic modernization, rather than the selection of an elite who will attempt (inevitably unsuccessfully) to monopolize information and knowledge.

Generalized knowledge, as indicated by Laborit, is what is required not only to establish the social purposes of modernization directed towards collective survival rather than competition at the expense of others, but also for the fullest use to be made of the new informating technology. To an extent this is already recognized by employers, who officially call for more generalized instead of specific skills from their employees. However, it has been suggested that employers are unwilling to allow the application of the new skills developed by the latest information technology to render transparent and accessible their own prerogatives of managerial control. Middle managers may be squeezed out, but top employers prefer to sustain the hierarchies in which they are advantageously placed, rather than to apply the technology to its fullest benefit for all, or even for their own firms. Only new companies in the few sectors of the economy still open enough to allow innovation (for example, in advertising or computer software) may for a time employ 'flattened' hierarchies, but as they become profitable they are likely to revert to traditional forms of management and control, even if they are not taken over by existing monopolies.

This is where the question of democracy comes in. It has also been suggested that new technology can be used to extend and develop democratic processes. Democratic control of schools and colleges, as of other public institutions, must be reasserted over the accountability through the market that 'free-market' philosophies advocate as the most efficient method of public accountability, increasingly substituting market mechanisms for democratic control. Exercises in democracy can be stimulated by education from an early age, while the extension of democracy to localities and regions can foster education and training around the economic and social regeneration of depressed areas. Rebuilding programmes on the most run-down estates, for example, can be used to develop building skills and knowledge under the control of and using the personal resources and experience of the residents.

In employment, workplace training committees (WTCs) should be made up of employee and employer representatives and have powers of co-determination with employers within enterprises, as in Germany. Powers of co-determination can then be raised at different levels and stages of social ownership. Initially WTCs can begin by conducting 'training audits' in their workplaces in the same way that environmental concerns may be registered. Such audits will be the basis upon which to develop internal training within enterprises, opening opportunities to all sections of the workforce and fostering a training culture by workers themselves training the trainees on the German *Meister* model. As in Germany, no firm over a given size should be able to trade without a qualified worker-trainer for every so many trainees at lower levels. In addition, worker-trainerships will help to provide a career ladder based upon skills. Firms can be encouraged to train young workers and retrain returnees in-house by grants, and there will have to be a training levy on employers per employee whether they train them or not. This reinstated levy–grant system will be nationally set but locally administered at the level of local labour markets, as well as across sectors nationally as the Industrial Training Boards used to do.

Job rotation should be established within enterprises as the principal means of generalizing information and sharing specialist knowledge to enhance real flexibility and progression. Secretaries, for example, as Randall Collins suggested,

> are in a perfect situation for on-job learning of managerial skills. At present the sex–caste barrier defines their positions as a separate enclave, however, so that virtually no secretary is ever promoted to take her boss's position. Nevertheless, this is not only technically feasible, but once was the standard promotion line. Before the late nineteenth century secretaries were males acting as apprentices for later administrative responsibility.
>
> (Collins, 1979, p. 200)

For Collins, this was just one example of 'job rotation across all existing lines of authority and specialization' by which 'all types of work would become subject to a common labour pool and respond to the same wage conditions' (p. 200), overcoming labour market segmentation. However, since this is unlikely to appeal to those with vested interest in sustaining their place in the existing hierarchy of knowledge and power, vocational education must be rescued from the marketplace, where it will always be low on employers' priorities. Instead of self-appointed little groups of local businessmen (almost invariably) on Training and Enterprise Councils, all public expenditure on education and training must be publicly reported and accounted for directly to democratically elected bodies.

Unlike in Germany, where a dual system separates the vocational from the academic at an early age (even if both routes enjoy more parity of esteem than they ever did or conceivably could in Britain), the first step to generalizing the knowledge upon which to inform democracy and modernization is to establish for as many people as possible the normality and desirability of full-time education to eighteen and recurring returns to learning full- and part-time thereafter. Here the example of the US community colleges, rather than the German model, can be followed. The normality of leaving general and usually full-time education or training at eighteen should also be used to emphasize the assumption of full citizenship rights and responsibilities from the age of eighteen, not twenty-five as has come to be increasingly the case. All young people should be brought in from the margins of society, instead of a section of them being relegated to a secondary labour market in the regions and inner cities. School or college leaving 'proms' at eighteen could be used to make this point and would be well received, since they are widely understood by young people brought up on a diet of American television and video culture.

Financial support should be available to students from the age of sixteen onwards in order to raise participation rates and the rate of return post-eighteen. The government set admirable targets for increasing numbers in higher education but contradicted them by introducing loans to pay for courses raised to their full cost. Predictably this will restrict access to higher education, for the market cannot deliver the mass higher education system, that is proposed. Loans must be abolished and the recommendation of the 1963 Robbins Report, of access to HE for all who can benefit from it, re-established. Nor should the definition of ability to benefit be dictated by arbitrarily rising academic entry standards; access must be increasingly opened to all who wish to enter their local college full- or part-time, in or out of paid employment.

For those in and out of employment, tertiary, further or adult colleges are well placed to become the linchpin of the new system of education and training. If the right of all school-leavers to enter their local college is guaranteed, progression from schools and adult education will facilitate access to higher education. Before the government cut further education, tertiary and sixth-form colleges loose into the marketplace, making planning and coordination difficult if not impossible, FE colleges in particular were well integrated with what remained of skill training in local labour markets through TVEI and other 'bridging' arrangements with their local secondary and special schools. They also increasingly franchise the lower levels of higher education courses from the institutions with which they are linked. Rather than degree courses being made shorter, as the government now proposes, the two years that many already spend in FE before moving on to higher education can become the basis for a new two-plus-two-year degree structure, the first two years to eighteen for standard-age entrants being a broad-based diploma or baccalaureat embracing both academic and vocational – or general and specific – skills. Proposals for such a unitary examination to end the division between education and training have already been published by the Institute for Public Policy Research. Many diplomates would move on, then or later in their careers, to take their study up to degree level with two further years full-time at higher education college, followed by two years of postgraduate study to master level.

Such a full-time educational entitlement will be expensive but it is a social priority that is required to raise the general level of information-handling ability among the population, which is necessary for modernization of the economy as well as to adapt to the accelerating pace of historical and even climatic change. The costs will be lessened by incorporating independent study into the learning programmes of all students, beginning as early as possible, by building upon the project work still widely undertaken in primary schools. Instead of a 'cramming' for tests that select a minority for entry to the next stage, the methods of learning and assessment associated with GCSE coursework before it was restricted by government should be raised from the schools through to further and higher education. This does not mean that students will study on their own – though they will do this as well, as new means of accessing information replace archaic forms of delivery, such as lectures. Rather, their individual programmes of study will include some element of original discovery, creation or research. Since many will be seconded from employment or on behalf of their local communities, these discoveries will return more then was invested in them, for creative artists, scientists or craftworkers (both art and science being crafts) are the only learners who give back more information than was entrusted to them by their education or training.

Investigation, experiment and debate by all students and as many other people as possible is vital today when so many received ideas in the social and natural sciences are open to question. In addition, new technology can be applied at every level of learning to facilitate routine memorization and to allow imagination free rein beyond the immediate necessity to earn a wage and the constraints of production for profit. It was Mrs Thatcher who made the point to the Parliamentary and Scientific Committee's fiftieth anniversary celebration that 'The greatest economic benefits of scientific research have always resulted from advances in fundamental knowledge rather than the search for specific applications.' This space within education for seeding new ideas must be preserved and extended by making scientific research and artistic creation an integral part of the independent study of all students, rather than separating teaching from research as the government now proposes.

Independent and individual study across traditional subject boundaries will be facilitated by the widely proposed and implemented modular systems of certification. These facilitate access through various modes of study at home and at work, and through the recognition of prior learning, and they enable credit accumulation and transfer. In a modular system, however, it is essential not to lose sight of the divisions between disciplines as well as the interrelations between them. It is important to distinguish between 'genuine' fields of study and practice corresponding to defined areas of reality, and outdated and arbitrary academic subject divisions, as for example in the 'national' curriculum, which only hinder thought and dampen discovery. While advances in knowledge often come from the imaginative projection from one frame of reference to another, this is not the same as a 'pick-'n'-mix' of modules from different areas of study. Guided only by vocational (i.e. labour market) choice, there is a loss of theoretical generalized knowledge in favour of specialized knowledge applicable only to occupational tasks not conceptually related to one another. At another level, modular higher education can also encourage the tendency towards 'educational consumerism' already evident in some universities, where students take 'interesting' and 'exciting' courses merely for their cultural cachet. Philosophical discussion, counselling and support are required if the modular method is not to degenerate into irrelevant educational consumerism at one end, combined with the myopic relevance of narrow vocational goals at the other. Nor should it become a way of just packing in and processing more students, as it already has in some former polytechnics.

To ensure that modular qualifications, while they are employment-related, are not employment-led, educational interests must have more influence in the National Council for Vocational Qualifications. Here again democratic accountability and control enters the frame, for the NCVQ should also be linked to the Workplace Training Committees, as recommended by the Trades Union Congress. Liaising with the WTCs, further and higher education colleges should also be responsible for the external skill-setting and validation needed to maintain national and European standards if skills are to be genuinely transferable between occupational sectors and different firms in the same sector throughout the EC. Universities and the other colleges and polytechnics that have followed them into the marketplace should all be brought back under local (city-wide or regional) democratic structures, so that they can play a full part in the regeneration of their localities. While teachers and lecturers at all levels, together with their students, have to have the academic freedom to pursue pure research at the generalized level that even Mrs Thatcher could see was necessary for scientific and cultural advance, their knowledge and skills must be relevant to the local communities that sustain them. Explaining their activities to people other than their peers could be a good exercise in communication for some engaged in more obscure research; after all, as Einstein said, 'If an expert cannot explain the basics of his subject to a layman in five minutes, then he is not an expert.'

The resources are available for the investment required if education and training are to play their part in a programme of economic modernization and social reconstruction. As stated by another semi-retired former minister, the last Labour Chancellor, Denis Healey, 'For Britain the first priority must be a massive switch from defence spending to economic reconstruction. Otherwise we cannot hope to repair the damage done in recent years to our economic infrastructure – our roads and railways, our schools and universities.' Such a redirection of resources can prepare the way for a culture of lifelong learning and recurrent access to further and higher education and adult training. The release of facilities in schools and colleges caused by the (temporary) demographic drop in the numbers of teenagers creates opportunities for providing education and training for the 70 per cent of the current workforce who have not acquired any worthwhile vocational qualification, as well as the three million people who are unemployed. With investment in the technology, schools and colleges could respond to the gathering pace of technological change, which requires a corresponding programme of retraining throughout employees' careers.

The subsidy of private schools through charitable status and the Assisted Places Scheme should be ended, as much to end the white flight and snobbery associated with the majority of them as to redistribute resources more fairly. The close connection of the elite minority of these schools with the antique universities could also be severed by turning the Oxbridge colleges into residential adult colleges, like Ruskin College in Oxford. This would be widely supported by the many adults who would then be given a chance to attend them. It would also nip in the bud the present moves towards setting up a super-league of semi-private elite institutions preserving their place at the top of the academic tree through marketing archaic and elite courses to those able to pay for them. The ending of the binary divide between universities and polytechnics plus colleges would not then result in a new division of higher education. Instead of the polytechnics now aping the universities, the original polytechnic vision of popular universities ought to be spread throughout the new unified higher education sector.

Similarly to the private schools, the few City Technology Colleges in which so much money has been invested with so little result can be reabsorbed into their local education authorities to service IT training in their neighbouring industry, as well as in the schools and colleges to where their pupils and teachers may return. It would have cost £3 billion to equip every secondary school in the country to the standard of the first CTC in Solihull; this sounds a lot but it is only a fraction of the still mounting cost of the Trident missile system.

These are all practical proposals that could be implemented now to begin to move towards the learning society that will be required in the future. Yet a redirection of resources to enable schools and colleges to provide all their students, as well as adults returning to and retraining for work, with the generalized knowledge necessary for full participation in a modernized and informated economy would still provide only the technical potential to create a new and unified system of education for work. A new curriculum, which facilitates instead of prevents transfer between its different levels, is also required.

Simply, education can no longer be about selection for the employment hierarchy. The 'needs' of industry have to be set in a wider framework of human and environmental need. To do this requires a greater contribution of generalized knowledge to work-related education and training. In particular, theory should be related to the specific life experiences of students and trainees – 'work experience' in a deeper sense than it usually carries. From this standpoint a progressive curriculum must lead on to an understanding of the organization of the economy as a whole and of the relationships of power and possession that are involved in it. Such a curriculum will insist on international connections, on understanding 'domestic' as well as paid employment and on opening for consideration the finality of social actions in relation to the larger political and ecological systems of which they are a part.

In a modernizing economy, education and training must raise the skills of all workers from the bottom up, much as campaigns in the Third World have aimed to raise literacy and numeracy rates. Education and training will then integrate rather then separate manual and mental labour. If education is to build the skills and knowledge base of society to take fullest advantage of the latest developments in technology, it must begin by recognizing how new technology has been applied during the economic restructuring of the past decade to deskill many of the tasks involved in production, distribution and services. A new division within the working population has been created, separating an 'underclass' stigmatized by the poverty that disenfranchises its members from equal participation in society. Resources will have to be specifically targeted at the poorest localities to overcome this disadvantage, reversing present priorities. New technology provides the potential to enable all working people to become multiskilled and flexible in a true sense, able to undertake a wide range of specific and general tasks, including self-management of their cooperative enterprises and democratic government of their society.

By not only simplifying tasks but sharing and integrating them, new technology can contribute, as has been indicated, to increasing productivity with less repetitive and laborious effort. It thus presents a historic opportunity to overcome the ancient division between workers by hand and workers by brain. This challenges the hierarchy of white over blue collars, of office over plant, managers over managed and those who think over those who do. This is certainly the logic of technical evolution and it should be used to unite workers who have been divided in other ways – through age, education, gender, race, region, etc. – against the few who control and benefit directly (as opposed to indirectly) from the continued and systematic exploitation of the vast majority of humankind and the destruction of our common environment.

In conclusion, Laborit's question of whether human beings are programmed by nature to be merely commodity producers must surely be answered in the negative. Unlike other species and previous civilizations we do not lack the information to predict or the means to redirect the course of our society. The real question is whether humanity can exercise its unique capacity to envision the future in order to open its present closed system to a level beyond its own self-destructive perpetuation. The contemporary collapse of previous attempts to overcome the vicious cycles of commodity production and imperial competition does not augur well for the effort that is necessary to learn the lessons of their failure. Yet this is what is now required for further progress and future survival.

Bibliography

Ainley, P. (1988) *From School to YTS: Education and Training in England and Wales 1944-1987*. Milton Keynes: Open University Press.
Ainley, P. (1990a) *Vocational Education and Training*. London: Cassell.
Ainley, P. (1990b) *Training Turns to Enterprise*. London: The Tufnell Press.
Ainley, P. (1991) *Young People Leaving Home*. London: Cassell.
Ainley, P. and Corney, M. (1990) *Training for the Future: The Rise and Fall of the Manpower Services Commission*. London: Cassell.
Amin, S. (1989) *Eurocentrism* (trans. R. Moore). New York: Monthly Review Press.
Annett, J. and Sparrow, J. (1983) *Transfer of Training, Basic Issues: Policy Implications – How to Promote Transfer. A Report for the Manpower Services Commission*. Coventry: Warwick University Department of Psychology.
Ashton, D., Maguire, M. and Spilsbury, M. (1990) *Restructuring the Labour Market: The Implications for Youth*. London: Macmillan.
Aulin, A. (1982) *The Cybernetic Laws of Social Progress*. Oxford: Pergamon Press.
Ballard, J.G. (1991) *The Kindness of Women*. London: Collins.
Bateson, G. (1978) *Steps towards an Ecology of Mind*. London: Paladin.
Bernstein, B. (1964) Social class, speech systems and psychotherapy. *Sociology*, **15**(1), 54-64.
Beveridge, W. (1909) *Unemployment: A Problem for Industry*. London: Longman.
Blackwell, T. and Seabrook, J. (1985) *A World Still to Win: The Reconstruction of the Post-war Working Class*. London: Faber.
Blumenberg, H. (1983) *The Legitimacy of the Modern Age* (trans. R. Wallace). Cambridge, MA: MIT Press.
Bourdieu, P. with Saint-Marin, M. (1976) Anatomie de goût. *Actes de recherche en sciences sociales*, 5 October, 2-112.
Brady, T. (1984) *New Skills in British Industry*. MSC Skills Series No. 5. Sheffield: MSC.
Braverman, H. (1974) *Labor and Monopoly Capital: The Degradation of Work in the Twentieth Century*. New York: Monthly Review Press.
Brown, E. and Senker, P. (1982) *Manpower Intelligence and Planning*. Sheffield: MSC.
Brown, P. and Scase, R. (eds) (1991) *Poor Work, Disadvantage and the Division of Labour*. Milton Keynes: Open University Press.
Burgess, T. (1986) *New Technology and Skills in British Industry*. MSC Skills Series No. 1. Sheffield: MSC.
Callinicos, A. (1989) *Against Postmodernism: A Marxist Critique*. Cambridge: Polity Press.
Centre for Contemporary Cultural Studies (1982) *The Empire Strikes Back: Race and Racism in Seventies Britain*. London: Hutchinson.
Clarke, J. and Jefferson, T. (1975) Working class youth cultures. Occasional Paper of the Centre

for Contemporary Cultural Studies, Birmingham University.
Coates, K. and Silburn, R. (1970) *Poverty: The Forgotten Englishman*. Harmondsworth: Penguin.
Cockburn, C. (1983) *Brothers: Male Dominance and Technological Change*. London: Pluto Press.
Cockburn, C. (1986) *Two Track Training*. London: Macmillan.
Coffield, F. (1990) From the decade of the enterprise culture to the decade of the TECs. *British Journal of Education and Work*, 4(1), 59-78.
Coffield, F. and MacDonald, R. (1991) *Risky Business? Youth and the Enterprise Culture*. London: Falmer.
Cohen, J. (1981) Can human irrationality be experimentally demonstrated? *Behavioural and Brain Sciences*, 4, 317-70.
Cohen, P. (1986) *Rethinking the Youth Question*. London: Institute of Education Post-16 Centre.
Coleman, R. (1988) *The Art of Work: An Epitaph to Skill*. London: Pluto Press.
Collins, H. (1989) *Artificial Experts, Social Knowledge and Intelligent Machines*. Cambridge, MA: MIT Press.
Collins, R. (1979) *The Credential Society: An Historical Sociology of Education and Stratification*. New York: Academic Press.
Cooley, M. (1975) Mental therbligs. *New Society*, 20 March.
Cooley, M. (1980) *Architect or Bee? The Human Technology Relationship*. Slough: Langley Technical Services.
Coopers & Lybrand (1991) *Managing for Manpower Shortage*. London: Coopers & Lybrand Deloitte.
Corney, M. (1991) Missing, a training strategy at the level of the individual firm. *Training Tomorrow*, May, 16-17.
Coulton, J. (1977) *Greek Architects at Work: Problems of Structure and Design*. London: Paul Elek.
Crompton, R. (1991) Three varieties of class analysis: a comment on R. E. Pahl. *International Journal of Urban and Regional Research*, 15(1), 108-13.
Curtis, S. (1952) *Education in Britain since 1900*. London: Dakers.
Daye, S. (1987) The black middle class. Unpublished PhD thesis, Aston University, Birmingham.
Dean, H. (1991) In search of the underclass. In P. Brown and R. Scase (eds), *Poor Work, Disadvantage and the Division of Labour*. Milton Keynes: Open University Press.
Dorin, G. (1989) The warming of the Earth. *OECD Observer*, February/March.
Douglas, M. (1986) *Risk Acceptability According to the Social Sciences*. London: Routledge.
Durkheim, E. (1979) *The Evolution of Educational Thought: Lectures on the Formation and Development of Secondary Education in France* (trans. P. Collins). London: Routledge.
Evans, B. (1992) *The Politics of the Training Market*. London: Routledge.
Fairley, J. (1990) *The MSC in Scotland*. Edinburgh: Edinburgh University Press.
Finn, D. (1984) Untitled draft submission to the National Labour Movement Enquiry into Youth Unemployment and Training. Unpublished.
Gallie, D. (1988) *Employment in Britain*. Oxford: Blackwell.
Gellner, E. (1983) *Nations and Nationalism*. Oxford: Blackwell.
Gimpel, J. (1983) *The Cathedral Builders* (trans. T. Waugh). London: Michael Russell.
Goldthorpe, J. (1980) *Social Mobility and Class Structure in Modern Britain*. Oxford: Clarendon Press.
Goldthorpe, J. and Lockwood, D. (1969) *The Affluent Worker in the Class Structure*. Cambridge: Cambridge University Press.
Gorz, A. (1982) *Farewell to the Working Class: An Essay in Post-industrial Socialism*. London: Pluto Press.
Green, A. (1990) *Education and State Formation: The Rise of Education Systems in England, France and the USA*. London: Macmillan.
Green, E. (1948) Education for citizenship. In H. Tracey (ed.), *The British Labour Party*, Vol. 2. London: Caxton.
Greenslade, R. (1976) *Goodbye to the Working Class*. London: Boyars.

Griffin, C. (1985) *Typical Girls*. London: Routledge.
Hakim, C. (1987) Trends in the flexible workforce. *Employment Gazette*, 11/87, pp. 546-60.
Hall, S. (1977) Marx's theory of classes. In A. Hunt (ed.), *Class and Class Structure*. London: Lawrence & Wishart.
Handy, C. (1984) *The Future of Work: A Guide to a Changing Society*. Oxford: Blackwell.
Harvey, D. (1989) *The Condition of Postmodernity: An Enquiry into the Origins of Cultural Change*. Oxford: Blackwell.
Hassan, J. (1988) Social class, disease and death: an essay in social medicine. *Proceedings of the Society for Hornpathology, Institute of Public Health, University of Tampere*.
HMSO (1943) *Report of the Committee of the Secondary Schools Examination Council, Curriculum and Examinations in Secondary Schools* (The Norwood Report). London: HMSO.
HMSO (1959) *Fifteen to Eighteen* (The Crowther Report). London: HMSO.
Hickox, M. and Moore, R. (1992) Education and post-Fordism: a new correspondence? In P. Brown and H. Lauder (eds), *Education for Economic Survival*. London: Routledge.
Hirschhorn, L. (1986) *Beyond Mechanization: Work and Technology in a Postindustrial Age*. Cambridge, MA: MIT Press.
Hobbs, D. (1990) *Doing the Business: Entrepreneurship, the Working Class and Detectives in the East End of London*. Oxford: Oxford University Press.
Hobsbawm, E. (1969) *Industry and Empire*. Harmondsworth: Pelican.
Hodges, A. (1983) *Alan Turing: The Enigma*. London: Hutchinson.
Hoggart, R. (1958) *The Uses of Literacy*. Harmondsworth: Penguin.
Hutson, S. and Jenkins, R. (1989) *Taking the Strain: Families, Unemployment and the 'Transition' to Adulthood*. Milton Keynes: Open University Press.
Institute for Public Policy Research (1990) *A British Baccalaureat: Ending the Division between Education and Training*. London: IPPR.
Jackson, B. (1964) *Streaming, an Education System in Miniature*. London: Routledge.
Jackson, B. and Marsden, D. (1962) *Education and the Working Class. Some General Themes Raised by a Study of 88 Working-Class Children in a Northern Industrial City*. London: Routledge.
Johnson, R. (1985) *The Politics of Recession*. London: Macmillan.
Jowell, R. and Brook, L. (eds) (1991) *British Social Attitudes Cumulative Source Book: The First Six Surveys*. Aldershot: Gower.
Kelman, J. (1989) *A Disaffection*. London: Secker & Warburg.
Knight, C. (1990) *The Making of Tory Education Policy in Post-war Britain 1950–1986*. Lewes: Falmer.
Kirchner, E., Hewlett, N. and Sobirey, F. (1984) *Report of the Social Implications of Introducing New Technology in the Banking Sector*. Luxembourg: Office for Official Publications of the European Communities.
Kohler, W. (1968) *Gestalt Psychology: An Introduction to New Concepts in Modern Psychology*. New York: Mentor.
Kumar, K. (1978) *Prophecy and Progress*. Harmondsworth: Penguin.
Kusterer, K. (1978) *Know-how on the Job: The Important Working Knowledge of 'Unskilled' Workers*. Boulder, CO: Westview Press.
Laborit, H. (1977) *Decoding the Human Message* (trans. S. Boddington and A. Wilson). London: Allison & Busby.
Labov, W. (1973) The logic of nonstandard English. In N. Keddie (ed.), *Tinker, Tailor . . . The Myth of Cultural Deprivation*. Harmondsworth: Penguin.
Landes, D. (1972) *The Unbound Prometheus: Technological and Industrial Development in Western Europe from 1750 to the Present*. Cambridge: Cambridge University Press.
Larkin, P. (1988) Annus mirabilis. In *Collected Poems*. London: Faber.
Leadbeater, C. (1989) In the land of the dispossessed. In L. McDowell, P. Sarre and C. Hamnett (eds), *Divided Nation: Social and Cultural Change in Britain*. London: Hodder & Stoughton.
Leavis, F. (1972) Hard Times: The world of Bentham. In F. Leavis and Q. Leavis, *Dickens the Novelist*. Harmondsworth: Pelican.

Lee, D. (1982) Beyond deskilling: skill, craft and class. In S. Wood (ed.), *The Degradation of Work? Skill and Deskilling and the Labour Process*. London: Hutchinson.

Lee, D., Marsden, D., Rickman, P. and Duncombe, J. (1990) *Scheming for Youth: A Study of YTS in the Enterprise Culture*. Milton Keynes: Open University Press.

London, J. (1903) *The People of the Abyss*. London: Isbister.

Lovering, J. (1989) A perfunctory sort of post-fordism: economic restructuring, spatial change and labour market segmentation in Britain in the 1980s. Paper for Work, Employment and Society Conference, University of Durham.

Lucie-Smith, E. (1981) *The Story of Craft: The Craftsman's Role in Society*. Oxford: Phaidon.

Lyotard, J. (1979) *The Post-Modern Condition: A Report on Knowledge*. Manchester: Manchester University Press.

McLean, I. (1989) *Democracy and New Technology*. Cambridge: Polity Press.

Mann, N. (1991) *The Making of an English 'Underclass': The Social Divisions of Welfare and Labour*. Milton Keynes: Open University Press.

Manpower Services Commission (1977) *Analytic Techniques for Skill Comparison*, Vols I and II. Sheffield: MSC.

Manpower Services Commission (1980) *Outlook for Training*. Sheffield: MSC.

Manpower Services Commission (1982) Youth Task Group Report. Sheffield: MSC.

Manpower Services Commission (1984) *Instructional Guide to Social and Life Skills*. Sheffield: MSC.

Manpower Services Commission (1985) *The Impact of New Technology on Skills in Manufacturing and Services*. Sheffield: MSC.

Martell, G. (1976) The politics of reading and writing. In R. Dale, G. Esland and M. McDonald (eds), *Schooling and Capitalism: A Sociological Reader*. Milton Keynes: Open University Press.

Marwick, A. (1980) *Class, Image and Reality in Britain and the USA since 1930*. London: Collins.

Marx, K. (1971) *Capital: A Critical Analysis of Capitalist Production* (trans. E. Aveling and S. Moore). London: Allen & Unwin (facsimile edition).

Massey, D. (1983) *Spatial Divisions of Labour: Social Structures and the Geography of Production*. London: Macmillan.

Mayr, O. (1986) *Authority, Liberty and Automatic Machinery in Early Modern Europe*. Baltimore: Johns Hopkins University.

Moore, R. (1985) *Education, Training and Production: A Critique of the Current Debate*. London: Polytechnic of the South Bank.

Morgan, E. (1973) *The Descent of Woman*. London: Corgi.

Morgan, K. and Sayer, A. (1988) *Microcircuits of Capital, 'Sunrise' Industry and Uneven Development*. Cambridge: Polity Press.

Moser, C. and Hall, J. (1954) Social grading of occupations. In D. Glass (ed.), *Social Mobility in Britain*. London: Routledge.

Murray, C. (1990) *The Emerging British UNDERCLASS*. London: Institute for Economic Affairs.

Naftulin, D., Ware, J. and Donnelly, F. (1973) The Doctor Fox lecture: a paradigm of educational seduction. *Journal of Medical Education*, 98, 630-5.

Nairn, T. (1988) *The Enchanted Looking Glass: Britain and Its Monarchy*. London: Radius.

National Union of Teachers (1990) *A Strategy for the Curriculum*. London: NUT.

Organisation for Economic Development and Co-operation (1981) *Information Activities, Electronics and Telecommunications Technologies*. Paris: OECD.

Offe, C. (1985) *Disorganized Capitalism: Contemporary Transformations of Work and Politics*. Cambridge: Polity Press.

Pahl, R. (1989) Is the emperor naked? Some questions of the adequacy of sociological theory in urban and regional research. *International Journal of Urban and Regional Research*, 13, 709-20.

Phillips, A. and Taylor, B. (1986) Sex and skill. In *Waged Work: A Reader*. Feminist Review edition. London: Virago.

Polanyi, K. (1946) *Origins of Our Time: The Great Transformation*. London: Gollancz.

Bibliography

Polanyi, M. (1962) Tacit knowing: its bearing on some problems of philosophy. *Review of Modern Physics*, 34(4), 601–16.
Polanyi, M. (1969) *Personal Knowledge: Towards a Post-critical Philosophy*. London: Routledge.
Polsky, J. (1971) *Hustlers, Beats and Others*. Harmondsworth: Penguin.
Popper, K. (1966) *The Open Society and Its Enemies*. London: Routledge.
Pye, D. (1968) *The Nature and Art of Workmanship*. Cambridge: Cambridge University Press.
Randall, C. (1992) *Training and Enterprise Councils – An Exercise in Illusion, Exclusion and Class Elision*. Centre for a Working World, discussion paper 6. Sheffield: Centre for a Working World.
Robbins, D. (1988) *The Rise of Independent Study: The Politics and Philosophy of an Educational Innovation, 1970–87*. Milton Keynes: Open University Press.
Robbins, D. (1991) *The Work of Pierre Bourdieu: Recognizing Society*. Milton Keynes: Open University Press.
Roberts, K. (1990) Draft of an unpublished paper for the Department of Employment.
Roberts, K., Cook, F. and Semeonoff, E. (1977) *The Fragmentary Class Structure*. London: Heinemann.
Robinson, E. (1968) *The New Polytechnics: The People's Universities*. Harmondsworth: Penguin.
Robinson, P. (1992) *Education and Training for Young People in the 1990s*. Campaign for Work Research Report, Vol. 4, No. 3. London: The Campaign for Work.
Rosenbrock, H. (1977) The future of control. *Automatica*, 13, 389–92.
Rosenbrock, H. (1990) *Machines with a Purpose: Challenging the View that 'In Science, Man Is a Machine'*. Oxford: Oxford University Press.
Rubinstein, W. (1987) *Elites and the Wealthy in Modern British History: Essays in Social and Economic Theory*. Brighton: Harvester.
Sartre, J.P. (1969) *Being and Nothingness: An Essay on Phenomenological Ontology* (trans. M. Barnes). London: Methuen.
Schilling, C. (1989) *Schooling for Work in Capitalist Britain*. Lewes: Falmer.
Scott, J. (1991) *Who Rules Britain?* Cambridge: Polity Press.
Sennet, R. and Cobb, J. (1973) *The Hidden Injuries of Class*. New York: Vintage Books.
Simmel, G. (1978) *The Philosophy of Money* (ed. D. Frisby, trans. T. Bottomore and D. Frisby). London: Routledge.
Sinfield, A. (1981) *What Unemployment Means*. London: Robertson.
Smith, A. (1776) *The Wealth of Nations*, Vol. 1. London: Strahan & Cadell.
Stewart, A., Prandy, K. and Blackburn, P. (1980) *Social Stratification of Occupations*. London: Macmillan.
Swann, B. and Turnbull, M. (1978) *Records of Interest to Social Scientists 1919–39: Employment and Unemployment*. London: HMSO.
Tawney, R. (1931) *Inequality*. London: Unwin.
Taylor, F. (1947) *Scientific Management*. New York: Harper & Row.
Townsend, P. *et al.* (1987) *Poverty and Labour in London*. London: Low Pay Unit.
Trevor-Roper, H. (1973) Address to the Joint Association of Classical Teachers, reprinted in the *Spectator*, 14 July.
Wallace, C. and Chandler, J. (1989) Some alternatives in youth training: franchise and corporatist models. Unpublished paper, Plymouth Polytechnic.
Washburn, S. (1978) Human behavior and behavior in other animals. *American Psychology*, 33, 405–18.
Westergaard, J. and Resler, H. (1976) *Class in a Capitalist Society: A Study of Contemporary Britain*. Harmondsworth: Penguin.
Whitty, G. (1983) Missing: a policy on the curriculum. In A. Wolpe and J. Donald (eds), *Is There Anyone There from Education? Education after Thatcher*. London: Pluto Press.
Williams, S. (1985) *A Job to Live: The Impact of Tomorrow's Technology on Work and Society*. Harmondsworth: Penguin.
Willis, P. (1977) *Learning to Labour: How Working Class Kids Get Working Class Jobs*. Aldershot: Saxon House.

Wilmott, P. and Young, M. (1957) *Family and Kinship in East London*. London: Routledge.
Wittgenstein, L. (1968) *Philosophical Investigations* (trans. G. Anscombe). Oxford: Blackwell.
Woodward, J. (1965) *Industrial Organisation: Theory and Practice*. Oxford: Oxford University Press.
Woolfson, C. (1982) *The Labour Theory of Culture: A Reexamination of Engels' Theory of Human Origins*. London: Routledge.
Wright, E. (1984) A general framework for the analysis of class structure. In E. Wright (ed.), *The Debate on Classes*. London: Verso.
Zuboff, S. (1988) *In the Age of the Smart Machine: The Future of Work and Power*. Oxford: Heinemann.

Name Index

Ainley, P. 23, 29, 32, 27, 44–5, 54, 55, 61, 64, 76
Amin, S. 66, 83
Annett, J. 11
Ashford, S. 59, 62
Ashton, D. 62, 64
Aulin, A. 51

Ballard, J. 19
Bateson, G. 1, 31, 50
Bell, D. 3, 58
Benn, Tony 33
Bernstein, B. 61
Beveridge, W. 35, 47
Blackwell, T. 29
Blumenberg, H. 7, 10
Booth, W. 27
Bourdieu, P. 14, 56–7, 59, 60–1, 80–1
Brady, T. 20, 37, 40
Braverman, H. 19, 23, 38
Brontë, Emily 36
Brown, E. 39
Brown, P. 60
Burgess, T. 20, 37, 40

Callinicos, A. 41
Carrott, Jasper 68
Chandler, J. 23, 75–6
Clarke, J. 36
Coates, K. 35
Cobb, J. 81
Cockburn, C. 20
Coffield, F. 73, 75
Cohen, J. 5
Cohen, P. 61
Coleman, R. 13, 15
Collins, H. 14, 22
Collins, R. 19, 89
Cooley, M. 9
Corney, M. 23, 44–5, 48, 64, 76

Coulton, J. 16
Crompton, R. 58
Curtis, S. 30

'Daley, Arthur' 74
Darwin, Charles 26
Daye, S. 66
Dickens, Charles 32, 77
Dorin, G. 51
Douglas, M. 14
Durkheim, E. 56, 79

Ebert, F. 16
Edwards, T. 55
Einstein, Albert 92
Engels, Friedrich 25, 26, 28, 72
Evans, B. 44

Fairley, J. 44
Finn, D. 21
Ford, Henry 19, 42, 43, 50
Forte, C. 67, 73
Fowler, Norman 87

Gallie, D. 20
Gellner, E. 15–16
Gimpel, J. 16
Goldthorpe, J. 27, 35, 39
Gorz, A. 35
Green, A. 17
Green, E. 30
Greenslade, R. 31
Griffin, C. 37

Hakim, C. 40
Hall, J. 57
Hall, S. 27
Handy, C. 23
Harvey, D. 41
Hassan, J. 50

100

Name Index

Hayek, F. 63
Healey, Denis 92
Heath, Edward 63, 82
Hegel, G. W. F. 26
Hickox, M. 76
Hilferding, R. 28
Hirschhorn, L. 22, 23, 38, 49, 53-4
Hobbs, D. 32, 73-4
Hobsbawm, E. 17, 32, 35
Hobson, J. 28
Hodges, A. 86
Hoggart, R. 33
Hutson, S. 60

Jackson, B. 31, 58
Jefferson, T. 36
Jenkins, R. 60
Johnson, P. 63
Johnson, R. 28
Joseph, Sir Keith 35, 56, 63-5

Kelman, J. 72
Keynes, J. 41, 75
Kirchner, E. 39
Knight, C. 31
Kohler, W. 7
Kumar, K. 38
Kusterer, K. 21

Laborit, H. 51-2, 83, 85, 86, 93
Labov, W. 61
Landes, D. 17, 28
Larkin, Philip 33
Leadbetter, C. 60
Leavis, F. 77
Lee, D. 69
Lenin, Vladimir Ilyich 18, 28, 52
Lockwood, D. 35
London, Jack 27
Lucie-Smith, E. 16
Lyotard, J. 41

MacDiarmid, Hugh 82
MacDonald, R. 73
McIlvanney, Hugh 67
McLean, I. 53
Major, John 45, 64, 67, 70, 76
Mann, N. 63, 65
Martell, G. 17
Marsden, D. 31
Marwick, A. 29, 31
Marx, Karl 7, 8, 18, 25-9, 31, 32, 41, 58, 59, 68, 71, 72, 74
Massey, D. 36
Mayhew, H. 27
Mayr, O. 22
Michelangelo 16
Moore, R. 11, 76
Morgan, E. 15
Morgan, K. 24
Moser, C. 57
Murdoch, Rupert 63
Murray, C. 63

Naftulin, D. 21
Nairn, T. 28
Neave, Airey 63
Nesbitt, Rab C. 70
Newton, Isaac 9

Offe, C. 42, 64

Pahl, R. 57
Phillips, A. 20
Plato 16, 30
Polanyi, K. 15, 25, 65
Polanyi, M. 7-8, 9, 12, 13
Polsky, J. 73
Popper, K. 7
Porter, Lady 67
Pye, D. 5-7, 21

Randall, C. 76
Rees-Mogg, Sir William 28
Resler, H. 59
Ricardo, D. 27
Robbins, D. 14, 55, 57
Roberts, K. 32, 44, 58, 68, 70
Robinson, E. 34
Robinson, P. 47
Rosenbrock, H. 5, 9
Rubinstein, W. 29

Sartre, J. P. 68
Sayer, A. 24
Scase, R. 60
Schilling, C. 30
Scorsese, Martin 74
Scott, J. 27, 29
Seabrook, J. 29
Senker, P. 39
Sennett, R. 81
Silburn, R. 35
Simmel, G. 76, 80-1
Sinfield, A. 35
Smith, Adam 15, 17-18, 27
Sparrow, J. 11
Stalin, Joseph 75
Stewart, A. 57
Stonier, T. 54
Sugar, Alan 77
Swann, B. 47
Swift, Jonathan 60

Tawney, R. 30, 31
Taylor, B. 20
Taylor, Frederick 18
Tebbit, Norman 87
Thatcher, Margaret 4, 25, 28, 29, 33, 35, 37, 44, 45, 56, 63, 64, 65, 70, 74, 78, 83, 84, 91, 92
Townsend, P. 62
Trevor-Roper, H. 17
Trotsky, Leon 59, 75
Trotter, D. 74
Trotter, R. 74
Turing, Alan 86
Turnbull, M. 47

Name Index

Wallace, C. 23, 75-6
Washburn, S. 13
Weber, M. 58
Westergaard, J. 59
Whitehouse, Mary 33
Whitelaw, William 64
Whitty, G. 16
Wilkinson, Ellen 30
Williams, Shirley 50
Willis, P. 36, 37

Wilmot, P. 33
Wilson, Harold 33
Wittgenstein, L. 5, 8, 12
Woodward, J. 20
Woolfson, C. 13
Wright, E. 59

Young, M. 33

Zuboff, S. 16, 22-3, 36, 38, 40, 49, 83

Subject Index

apprenticeship   5, 11-12, 15, 16, 22, 34, 36, 46, 48, 49, 78, 80, 87, 89
aristocracy   27, 56
   'labour aristocracy'   28
art   3, 6, 9, 13, 16, 34, 47, 76-7, 88, 90
automation   22-3, 34, 37, 49

bourgeoisie   26, 68, 75, 83
   petit bourgeoisie   26-7, 66, 74-5, 76

capitalism   3, 41-2, 51, 52, 62, 71, 72, 73, 74, 75, 83
   state capitalism   1, 52, 72
caste   15, 28
charity   65
charters   76
class   39, 49, 50, 56, 57-61, 67-72, 83-4, 87
   Marxist concept   25-7
   middle   26, 41, 58, 59, 61, 67, 69-70, 77-9
      black   66
      'new'   59, 71
   upper (ruling)   27, 28-9, 56-7, 59, 62, 69, 71, 72, 80, 83
   working   3, 28, 29, 32-3, 35, 36-7, 40, 41, 42, 58, 59, 61, 62, 64, 67-70, 74, 79, 83-4
      'respectable' as opposed to 'rough'   34, 42, 65, 70
'classlessness'   4, 31, 33, 49, 62, 80, 83
clerical work, see office work
communism   1, 2, 18, 26, 32, 52, 75, 82-3
   Communist Manifesto   26
   Communist Party   59, 75, 84
computers   9, 10, 13, 17, 23, 24, 40, 50, 52-4, 57, 73, 75, 77, 88
consumerism   24, 55, 56, 58, 70, 76, 91
contract culture   23, 40, 55, 65, 73-5
core-periphery employment patterns   3, 23, 24, 38, 40, 42
craft   5, 8, 13, 16, 17, 20, 21, 22, 36, 37, 48, 84, 90

crime   73, 74
Crowther Report (1959)   24
culture   5, 13, 14, 20, 22, 34, 43, 47, 50, 56, 61, 68, 71, 79, 80-1, 85, 89, 92

democracy   2, 23, 41, 52, 53, 54, 55, 66, 83, 85, 87, 89, 91, 93
division of labour   14-15, 18, 84; see also gender; manual as opposed to mental labour; race; skill

education   7, 15, 16, 17, 21, 24, 29-32, 34, 36, 39, 44, 46, 47-8, 54-5, 56, 59, 64, 71, 72, 75, 76, 77-81, 85, 86-93
Education Act 1944   29
Education Act 1987   78
Education Reform Act 1988   17, 31, 33, 48, 49, 55, 64, 65, 78, 79, 87
employers   11, 19, 20, 22, 40, 41, 44, 45, 46, 48, 49, 57, 59, 71, 72, 75, 87, 88
   small   72-5
engineering   20, 22, 38, 46, 53
Enlightenment, the   2
environmental problems   1, 51-3, 66, 77, 82, 84-5, 86, 93
European Community   29, 53, 81-2, 87, 91

factories   3, 17, 19, 23, 41, 42, 54, 58, 84
fascism   66
feudalism   26, 27, 28
flexibility   22, 23, 38, 40-1, 42, 49, 74, 80, 89
franchising   23, 55-6
freedom   2, 7, 52, 83

gender   14-15, 20, 24, 30, 36, 37, 38, 39, 40, 41, 42, 45, 46-7, 58, 61, 89, 93

habits   6, 12, 14, 24
handicraft, see craft
housing   42, 45, 60, 73, 75, 88

103

Subject Index

imperialism   28, 48, 56, 66, 82–3, 84, 85, 93
independent study   55, 90–1
industrial revolution   3, 9, 17, 28, 48, 49
Industrial Training Boards   44, 89
informal or 'black' economy   73–4
information   9, 23, 41, 49, 54, 84, 86
    'information society'   3, 24, 38–9, 50–6

knack of acquiring a skill   12–13, 20, 21
knowledge   8, 86, 88, 89, 91, 92, 93
    tacit   7–8, 23

'labour aristocracy'   28
Labour Party and government   28, 29, 30, 31, 32, 33, 35, 41, 49, 64, 78
language   13, 61
leisure   24, 53
literacy   17, 24
love   8

managers and management   9, 21, 22, 23, 24, 27, 38, 39, 40, 41, 50, 53, 59, 76, 88, 89, 93
Manpower Services Commission   11, 12, 19, 34, 38, 44–5
manual as opposed to mental labour   8–9, 14, 16, 18, 23, 34, 35, 37, 38, 39, 40, 49, 54, 58, 59, 62, 68, 69, 70, 79, 84, 93
mass media   32, 42, 47, 54, 58, 63, 65, 66, 67–8, 71, 74, 82
mathematics   9–10, 76
medicine   9, 19
meritocracy   2, 87
mixed economy (new)   23
monarchy   28
money   76–7

'national' curriculum   55, 91
National Vocational Qualifications   11–12, 48, 91
nationalism   15, 17, 32, 64, 71, 81–2
needs   50
Neolithic revolution   14
new technology   3, 7, 10, 20, 21, 22, 37–8, 40, 42, 45, 46, 48–9, 52–3, 54, 55, 60, 66, 69, 80, 84–5, 87, 91, 92, 93
Norwood Report (1943)   29–30

Occupational Training Families   11, 12
office work   18, 19, 23, 24, 36, 38–9, 42, 50, 58, 60, 69, 87, 89, 93

opinion polls and 'public opinion'   59–60, 68, 69, 83

'post-Fordism'   3, 23, 40–1, 42, 58
post-modernism   3, 4, 7, 40, 58
poverty   35, 36, 62, 63, 70–1, 80, 93
professionalism   15, 19, 22, 24, 28
professions   19, 28, 36, 57, 60, 78, 79
proletarianization   27

race   32, 36, 41, 45, 62, 64–5, 71, 84, 93
Robbins Report (1963)   34, 90
robots   13, 24, 42, 54

science   1, 3, 7, 10, 13, 17, 26, 33–4, 47, 51, 55, 76, 84, 88, 90–1, 92
self-employment   73–5
'service class', *see* class: middle: 'new'
services   3, 23–4, 35, 36, 38–9, 42, 58, 69
skill shortages   13, 43, 44–6, 48, 49
skills   4, 5–9, 11, 12, 20, 24, 30, 34, 36, 37, 38, 40, 42, 43, 59, 65, 75, 84, 89, 93
sociology   1, 25, 37, 47, 57–60, 61–2, 63, 68, 69, 72, 84
state capitalism   1, 5, 72
status   57, 58, 60, 61, 83
systems theory   13, 22, 51, 77, 93

technicians   3, 13, 20, 22, 34, 37, 40, 46
technology   1, 14, 20, 22; see *also* new technology
tools   6, 7–8, 10, 51
trade unions   11, 19, 35, 40, 41, 49, 91
training, *see* education
Training and Enterprise Councils   44, 45–6, 89

uncertainty   6, 8, 9, 13, 21–2
'underclass'   27, 37, 40, 41, 43, 62–6, 70–1, 74, 80, 84, 93
unemployment   2, 12, 34–5, 36, 37, 40, 43, 44, 45, 46, 47, 49, 62–6, 70, 71, 73, 74, 83, 87
Utopia   52–3

work and work study   5–7, 10, 16, 18–19
worker cooperatives   54
Workplace Training Committees   88–9, 91

youth   33, 45, 61, 64, 66, 68, 89
Youth Training   12, 45, 47, 65, 68–9, 78, 87